AF407217

SAMKHYA AND GOLDEN MEAN
(The space of Analysis in the age of revelation of form)

Miguel Iradier

Index

SAMKHYA AND GOLDEN MEAN
(The space of Analysis in the age of revelation of form)

Miguel Iradier

SINOPSIS

SAMKHYA AND GOLDEN MEAN
(The space of Analysis in the age of revelation of form)

This book is basically about philosophy. Samkhya, which is the oldest Indian philosophy, had a decisive influence on the development of Buddhism. We will use its viewpoints to tackle a wide-ranging physical and mathematical question, related to the asymmetric principle of measurement established and generalised by Alexey Stakhov, founded on the mathematical principles of the Golden Mean or Continuous Proportion, which is commonly designated by the letter *phi (Φ)*.

The Samkhya is an exact, mathematical philosophy, which studies that waves and fluctuations of any kind of motion, with the mind considered as merely another form or order of motion in general. Samkhya means *proportion, measure* or *analysis.* Usually, the purpose of Samkhya is self- observation or the direct perception of the fluctuations of one'*s* own mind, with a view to achieving balance and an eventual end to its motion. Samkhya is thus the philosophical base that underlies yoga. However, although Samkhya generally focuses on direct perception or discrimination on the mind by attention or awareness, it is a universal theory or framework for the generality of the nature of motion, based on the concept of *modification* or *fluctuation.* Any modification of regular motion exists in three modalities or *gunas*: *Sattwa*, *Rajas* and *Tamas*. With *Tamas* as inertia, *Rajas* as action or mutation and *Sattwa* as the relative balance or equilibrium between the former two, or the joint sensitivity of the system, all three modalities can be matched perfectly with Newton's three principles of mechanics, which define rest or inertia, force and action–reaction. However, Newton's three principles oust the modality, as we can see particularly clearly in the third principle or law, which, being immediate, defines no *medium* for action–reaction, thereby making the *real* or specific transmission of communication or information impossible. Indeed, information is produced when the reaction of a system is *not equal* to the action received, i.e. when there is asymmetry and also a lack of temporal synchronicity. Newton's absolute time is an implicit principle of *global synchronisation,* which has persisted in the theory of relativity and quantum mechanics. A summary of this topic can be found in Koichiro Matsuno's online paper *Information: Resurrection of the Cartesian Physics.* Global synchronisation or absolute time is at best a metaphysical statement, although it has made our idea of physics and its constants possible. This absolute time means exactly the same in Newton's three laws, albeit in a different order, as the absolute awareness or *Purusha* of Samkhya with respect to the three modalities or *gunas.* But study of asymmetry or asynchrony between action and reaction is an ideal subject for the application of the Golden Mean or Continuous Proportion.

Samkhya may coincide with mechanics in its idea of the oscillator. The only empirical science derived from Samkhya that we are aware of is pulse- based medical diagnosis or *nadi vigyan,* where the pulse is a non-linear or non-analytical biological oscillator. Samkhya, however, is non-linear analysis *par excellence.*

The three *gunas* or modalities of Samkhya, when applied to the pulse oscillator, become the three *doshas* or humours of *ayurveda* and *nadi vigyan: Pitta, Vata* and *Kapha.* Since *Pitta* is equivalent to action or force, and *Kapha* to inertia or retention, *Vata,* as a principle of action and reaction, is the sensitivity of the balance between both. This strict correspondence is appropriate in relation to the moments of dynamics, although we have performed a transposition to a non-linear order that cannot be quantified as precisely, given the interdependence of the terms.

Pulsology was the first semiology to achieve both internal and experimental consistency, in a way that numerous modern attempt have been unable to equal. Pulsology, as morphology for diagnostic purposes, identifies between five essential properties of the pulse: rhythm, frequency, intensity, amplitude and *form*. The first four mean much the same as they do in harmonic or wave analysis, but the fifth has a unique meaning that is only found in morphology. It is a genuine, elusive *quintessence* that cannot be reduced to analytical interaction between the other four, and best expresses the non-linearity of the system, including an synthesising the full complexity of all the potential pairings between miscellaneous cycles that could affect this apparently isolated pulse. The *form* of the pulse is *not* just the irregularity of its wave compared with that of a harmonic oscillator; it is also a *thickness* characteristic of its plot or signature that can be translated into a buffering or lack of determination that is a *characteristic* of the *form* of the pulse, rather than a mere lack of determination considered as the incompleteness of the information available to us in this regard. Until recently, the *form* of the pulse could not be recorded by any mechanical detector, but could only be perceived by the direct sensitivity of the fingers of the *vadya* or examining doctor. Now, however, it can be captured properly by small laser diodes and also studied acoustically. Thus, it is now possible to study and analyse this *form* in real time under variable conditions.

We consider this *form* to be a universal characteristic of *all* motion, not only the pulse; all that has happened is that mechanics and analysis have ignored on a matter of pure principle. We may therefore be dealing with something that is of great importance that demands its own independent method.

The *preliminary* measurement of the three modalities tends to be rather imprecise because of the interdependence of terms mentioned above; they can only be considered as statistical proportions or weights of fuzzy sets within an expert system that can, at the same time, be considered as a control system. These fuzzy sets may be related to the Golden Mean at the intersection of sets — with the Golden Mean as a ratio of ratios, it must naturally correspond to these intersections or overlaps of fuzzy sets resulting from areas of inference applied to the curve of a graph. Several studies have already been done of the relationship between fuzzy sets and the Golden Mean. Nevertheless, this remains a purely heuristic, empirical approach, lacking any well-defined theoretical concept, although it may lead us towards some interesting ideas. In any case, it is possible to define a genuine theoretical model.

We do not believe that a force applied independent of time can exist in nature. In any case, the **impulse** seems more real to use as a fundamental unit. The impulse, conceived as force by time, as well as a variation of the moment, fully matches the notion of modification in Samkhya. A balance between impulses can, in turn, be conceived as an impulse with its own temporal dimension, if we fit into our imaginary balance an adjustment time between successive operations of removing and adding weights — a time to which we can also ascribe variability. Thus, we can conceive motion and velocity as balance between impulses in different or opposite directions, equalling not only the inertia and force in the wave of the pulse, but also the third principle of action and reaction, in the actual modality of the sensitivity of the balance. This estimate of the time interval between discrete operations now gives us a measure of the inertiality of the balance as a medium or instrument, or, if one prefers, its sensitivity. The three modes now share a time element, whereby both the mass and the force can be equalled with the impulse by means of the sensitivity of the balance. It should be noted that since the sensitivity of the balance can be computed as inertiality (although not immediately), we obtain a definition of the recursive or self-recurrent impulse, of the same nature as the Golden Mean itself. There are also certain clearly defined logical rules for the sequentiality of this self-recurrence, which are touched upon in the paper. Time itself can be defined as the actual and potential supply of operations within an interval; the possible operations are limited by the current loads and the available weights, which may differ in their magnitude and proportion, and which become optimal in generalisations of the classical problem of Fibonacci's weights. But it is the *form* of the pulse, the thickness or plot of its signature, that fits the possible solutions and *defines the relevant range of precision.* This is the key point, since there is no exact motion outside differential calculus, and all motion —classical or quantum— must have its own degree or plot of precision, inasmuch as none is purely linear or ideal.

In physics there are no *natural* units of energy, force or even mass, if we assume that pure inertia cannot be computed. Moreover, nor can we give any content to the notion of the cycle, which is reduced to the mere formality of the circle, and since Planck's action quantum is a unit of energy per cycle per second, we have no idea of what kind of recurrence this cycle corresponds to, which is overlooked when the unit is defined. Obviously, a cycle with no content or a purely formal cycle would only exist in the absolute absence of mass, which is not the case with any particle in motion. Owing to the recursive definition of the impulse, having been able to find an equivalence with mass or inertia, force and specific action–reaction, we can do the same with other magnitudes or notions, such as pressure, tension and many other existing or totally new ones. We will also find contents for the notion of the cycle as a recurrence. Why? For the same reason that we can make new definitions for numbers with their corresponding number theories within the golden system of numbering as conceived by Bergman and generalised by Stakhov. This seems barely credible. We have a universal translator of notions and units; and not only for known ones but also for any others we might come up with. This covers a wide range of different spheres that would not appear to be in contact with one another, from physics to psychology, via biology, economics and many others.

What is more, this physical principle of translation by material implication is inherently linguistic, and inevitable also covers all the possibilities of human languages. The three modalities can readily be associated with the subject, verb and predicate of our sentences. The same Continuous Proportion and modalities exist as connective and disjunctive functions, with an intermediate term in the *–and*-and *–or*-to allow for mixing and separation. In this paper the only non-rhetorical characterisation of nature is considered to lie in "joining and splitting", which only makes sense in relation to inequality, rather than for the equivalences and identities predicted by equations. Yet we also have Fibonacci's "words" and "strings", as logical sequences, which allow the transfer between content and form in the maximum possible number of orders of construction. "String" or "link" is one of the primary meanings of the word *guna*; meanwhile, the theory of golden numbers and the principle of asymmetric measurement closely related to them is the most efficient analogue–digital converter that we have found. Thus, we can linguistically access the pulse or any other motion with as much property as can be achieved through mathematics, which in this sense is considered as just another language, rather than a privileged one. This assertion in no way an exaggeration, and it may even be possible to demonstrate it, although we have neither the space nor the skill to deal with it in depth. The languages of nature, and their motion, are not just a metaphor, although they exist in metaphor: mathematics also has its own transformation space. Yet the density of a language hinges on its material implication, in the same way that mathematics only seems to become transcendent through its relationship to physical reality. However, all this is much too noble and serious to be turned into a simple formal game. We have no wish to add more storeys onto the Tower of Babel nor deepen the moat at its feet. Moreover, all this leads in the opposite direction to that of formal artifices, and Patanjali himself, the supreme summariser of Samkhya, pointed this out quite adequately: the sense of any language exists in its own right in the gap that separates the three moments, thus confirming that Samkhya is the true analysis, with mathematical analysis taking the opposite direction — that of composition. It is worth making the effort to comprehend this fully.

The true root of translation is motion itself, the *own form* of the motion, which has not until now been taken into account. Form and motion are the same thing: form cannot be conceived as being external or unspecific. If the phrase "the medium is the message" became famous for its ambiguity, we can be equally sure that with respect to motion *form is content,* and the more layers of ambiguity we remove, the truer this becomes. These layers are hidden in the very idea of exactitude that we apply to differential analysis, which does nothing but export problems to further spaces for abstraction — in order to remove ambiguity, precisely. But the fit, whether it is ambiguous or not, belongs to the form itself, and in this property ambiguity would just be irrelevant. Since our idea of "limit" and "function" refers to an irreducible morphological component, we can assume the unity of design and intent, i.e. understand through the motion itself the impossibility of fully separating efficient causes from final ones, or material from formal ones. Without this, there can be no theory of real-time evolution, but just an imaginary appeal to statistics and possible or past worlds. **The question boils down to this: we are now in a position to extract more, better information from the form of motion than of structures, with the justification for the latter being the shape of the motion itself. Furthermore, this allows the same information to be folded or synthesised. This remains valid at all levels.** By "structures" we mean whatever is intended to be free of conditioned motion and fixed by the resolution of the analysis, whether we are dealing with genes, conventional non-analytical curves or normal differential equations.

I am not a physicist or a mathematician, which is why I am raising this problem for anyone who is interested in it or capable of addressing it. The problem would seem to be related to the perturbation theory applied to an oscillator — but here we have a recursive or self-referencing definition, as well as a level of adjustment for precision or lack of determination in optimal terms of maximums and minimums within the actual *form* of the motion. This has never been suggested, and if it is understood, it could lead us to a completely new space for analysis. This is why I have subtitled this paper "The analysis space in the age of the discovery of form".

Naturally, we cannot expect to find any analytical solutions here, by positioning ourselves beyond the limits of differential calculus. The usefulness of all this is that non-analytical solutions for such systems take us to a new level of description to allow *translation between different systems*, as well as any possible redefinitions within a given system. The scope for this is too great for us to determine even within formal systems, but it can also transcend them via its capacity to redefine our actual concept of unity. What we lose in the general representation of nature, a mere surplus, we can gain in the capacity for real-time integration at all levels, including computing and work time. The new organisational power that resides here cannot be missed. In all our models representation it is either or question or it is ineffective — a mere obstacle. That said, all the excesses of abstraction to the point of unrecognisability are a consequence of this representational component.

We think that all the problems of contemporary physics related to the scalar component of fields pose the same difficulties as what we are dealing with here: the Higgs field for the masses of particles, the *lambda* tension constant or cosmological constant for the "weight" of space closely related, and even "dark mass" or probably inexistent dark matter. All of this leads to a break in the symmetry of our equations and the conditionality of their structure. We now find that that vector forces independent of local time have nowhere to rest and nothing to which they can be applied, and they are thus revealed to be largely fictitious. This could shatter the idea of the physical constant. Curiously, this scalar component of fields is also designated by the letter *phi (Φ)*, and in a context of adjusting functions with optimal local values. Meanwhile, some physicists, such as El Naschie have proposed focusing and unifying all physics on the constant *phi*; such attempts would appear to us to be far too speculative, since they are based on transfinite Cantorian spaces that make constructive procedures impossible. The mathematics of harmony driven by Stakhov is based on living priority to constructive definitions and limiting the inflation of imaginary, abstract spaces. This direction is one that merits further study, since too much emphasis now tends to be placed on complex space, with little understanding of real space and its degrees of compossibility.

But our problem is much more basic and general than the ones being addressed at the cutting edge of physics, which are the end result of extreme specialisation. One may think that we could not have chosen a more fragile motif than our balance to point out the stability of processes and things. But is stability guaranteed anywhere? We do not think it is, and the misunderstanding is based on both prejudice in favour of approaches with differential mathematical solutions and our idea of the mechanical, which always refers to inertia and rest as pure nothingness. The principle of minimal action may be the only reference for stability; but it is precisely differential calculus that has deprived this principle of the attention that it is due. There is no stability — only degrees of equilibrium. The contrary would only be possible if the mass and inertia were identical, in which case the mass would be zero and equivalent to rest; but this makes no sense at all, especially for physics, because for dynamics the mass is the point of reference and reality, having removed all properties of reference from rest. This sums up our concept of mechanics, and reductionism itself. Thus, mass can only be described in terms of non-linear motion, i.e. motion with its own *form*. This is the only way to be fully consistent with mechanicism; anything else is running away from the problem. Everything therefore depends on how the conditions are arranged: Samkhya is the doctrine of pure conditionality in nature, often expressed as the claim that "nothing exists on its own", but only in terms of its relationships and contrasts with other things.

As history has shown us, nature and the form of motion is one of the most general topics dealt with in philosophy. It can properly include both the mind and beauty, because beauty, first and foremost, is also motion, at times evidently so and at others only in deeply hidden form. Meanwhile, *phi*, the simplest ratio of recursivity or self-reference, leads us — thanks to its adherence to the singularity of things — to the ultimate problem at hand, the frame of reference, the most inexcusable and esoteric of all. Where is it, if intellect is, like *phi*, pure adherence? Although we have always dealt with reality, we have tended to confuse it compulsively with our arbitrary demarcations and definitions. This is the final link that is being dissolved.

The frame of reference and its definition are now in our hands but, more than ever before, all will depend on our intention to insert into reality.

SAMKHYA AND GOLDEN MEAN

(The space of Analysis in the age of revelation of form)

§ 1 §

Why we say about something that is "simply mechanic"? A simple harmonic oscillator, a pendulum without friction, is something easy to understand. To construct real pendulums fit to that ideal entails increasing degrees of difficulty and complexity. The simplicity of mechanics resides properly in its idea, more than in some manifest property of the things. An ideal mechanical system is only a limit for real systems; to turn ourselves into an inert system subject to mechanical forces involves the idea of the death. Besides and by definition we do not know any force at all that could be not mechanical nor subject that could not be inert at the moment of receiving it. No later extension of the physics has altered this fundamental conception, nor could at least imagine how to do it. The invisible nexus of the causality can be stumped, but it cannot be cut: otherwise we would be already outside of mechanics. Therefore, the idea of mechanics would be identical with the one of the ideal causality, that occurs in a single and same plane; in this item the program of pure reductionism would be condensed implying nothing else than another ideal, another limit for the last remission of the phenomena, no matter how varied could be the levels or emergencies of events. That unique and same plane in which all the forces, their actions and reactions would be developed, is not other one that the ideal plane by which

[23]

it rolls perfectly a smooth ball with total monotony that generates the inertia definition in Galileo and in Newton later. Like first of its variants, also the gravity was conceived originally like circular motion around the centre of grave bodies, now accelerated, in the famous experiment of the inclined plane.

This it is the beginning of the mechanics, also called dynamics, and of course that seems something too fundamental. Anyway, we know that in the meantime the uniform motion has been equaled with rest, and because of this, any characterization of a point in rest in the real space has been made impossible in other terms that those of dynamics or of the motion itself. From they arise here, then, all the difficulties around the reference systems that have been constituted in the problem par excellence of physics, with questions such as the weight of the vacuum and the generation of the mass of particles. I will not solve it, although one can only think that it would be more consequent with dynamics to assume that real space does not exist anymore, and that this space is not but a group of parameters for the adjustment of a temporary function. To assume this would surely require watching towards the sea that

breaks against the border of the differential calculus; but mainly, it would require watching towards uniform motion more like a destination than a point to begin with.

§ 2 §

To contemplate uniform motion or even the rest as destination would require seeing it from within. But it not exist a defined point where the external begins to be internal. Let us take the definition that gives Patanjali of the mental substrate during the gradual concentration in the meditation:

Tatah punah santoditau tulia-pratiaiau cittasiaikagrata-parinamah, Which can be translated: "the concentration takes place when the mental waves that rise and fall at two different moments are exactly equal." This is the definition of a simple

[24]

oscillator, or an inert ball that rolls on an ideal plane. What for us, seen from outside, has the full aspect of inanity, what makes think us irremediably about a flat encephalogram, it is for Samkhya the beginning and the condition of the most perfect life in awareness, and therefore, of the most perfect life also. For nobody escapes that a maintained attention is required to maintain that state; an attention that is more and more difficult to obtain for us nowadays. Who said inertia? What was about something "simply mechanic"?

§ 3 §

Samkhya, attributed to *rishi* Kapila, and exposed with insurmountable concision by Patanjali, is the philosophy that underlies and defines *yoga*: yoga is the cessation of the fluctuations of the mind. Or, in a more progressive form, the whole transit that leads to the arrested state. Therefore, it simply includes everything, since mind is also a mere object and a mere object of knowledge like all the others, although less graspable in appearance. To understand it: the objects or are not only pervaded or surrounded by our mind, but, being our mind only another kind of object, objects themselves have to exhibit mental properties, being knowables. The mind is the order of the fluctuations, and everything with fluctuations will participate necessarily in it. The consciousness or pure awareness by definition is not an object and therefore it does not show qualities. Nor it is an attribute of life, and for that reason it is beyond life or death; of inertia, of the forces or their reactions or fluctuations. Only assuming this we are free from absurd, anthropic principles and other perplexities. For the modern scientific mentality, dominating over any other one, the problem is how the things have begun to move from a rest that is excluded by definition and it becomes a non-being; for the perspective of Samkhya, that is not alien to the traditional and pre-scientific perspective in general, the things and beings have been moving always —for that reason they are actually beings—, and the only thing that is possible to contemplate is their possibilities of return to non-being and to the rest beyond

[25]

the fluctuations of the time. For one and another, motion is the problem and the solution is rest.

§ 4 §

Samkhya, as the study of the fluctuations of the mind that possibly can be lead to the rest, is an oscillator theory. But the qualities or moments that Samkhya detects in the fluctuations cannot be purely extrinsic, but internal or inherent, the discernment that only characterize them is realized inasmuch the mind is contemplated or testified by the consciousness with no qualities. There is not contradiction here, but continuity, since the motion characteristic of mind in its steps to acquisition of knowledge results from the same number of steps towards rest and therefore relative or tangential contact with the same knowledge as source. We will see that this break in continuity is the subject par excellence of Samkhya in any possible approach.

§ 5§

Between the varied meanings and possible translations of the term samkhya we have those of *analysis, detailed scrutiny, number, measurement and proportion.* The analysis that practices Samkhya is purely discriminative and intellectual, and in such sense it would be necessary to consider it objective. On the other hand the discrimination or *viveka* is made basically on an internal object, the mind, without another contour or profile that the one that conscience or consciousness can give it. Again, it is necessary here to give some explanations. For us, an object without external profile is only subjective, although only by the deformations that we have imposed on such conventional terms. Even so, this would not be a problem for Samkhya, which defines the supreme state of knowledge like the suppression of the same object and the "objective consciousness" in the sense that commonly we give

[26]

him. This is remarkable. In the continuity wake that leads to this knowledge, the data and the apperception in general must be of a more and more internal order. Well, even so, throughout the whole scale of the conceivable objects, from most external to the most internal, which is irreducible at the end of the analysis of the fluctuations are the three *gunas*, ultimate qualities or modalities of the conditioned nature, constituent and inherent to such fluctuations. We can understand by conditioned nature all nature now considered as manifestation —which already is inherent and coordinated as *gunas*—, now considered material or not (what it would be just an opinion), now perceivable or not. The conditioned nature is the order or inherent disorder to those fluctuations; when the three modalities reach the total equilibrium also cease the fluctuations and the order or disorder of manifestation.

§ 6 §

Gunas, the moments or modalities of nature, can admit an extensive or an intensive breakdown, they can be explicit or implicit, but in no case they leave their inherency, what is to say that they are not susceptible of later analysis. They mark the end of the analysis, and therefore any consideration or contemplation on them begins where the analysis finishes. This has to be worth for which now we understand like mathematical analysis and also for everything what studies physics like intrinsic of the differential calculus. The break or the continuity is not marked by one theory or another one, but the same application of the calculation when it lets find solutions or these are multiplied becoming irrelevant; it is well-known that is enough three variables or three independent bodies in a problem to throw to us fully in non-linear dynamics. The non-linear thing is the non-proportional thing; the sense of the proportion in Samkhya aims towards that apparent lack of proportionality. The three *gunas* are different, they are the different thing par excellence for the discernment, and nevertheless they only can exist by its mutual correlation; in the same way in the non-linear analysis the difference

[27]

between dependent and independent variables begins to become semantic and tends to become an open question in dependency of the posing and the solutions. If we took the famous three-bodies-problem, only by the initial posing we could say that those bodies are independent; what decides the question is the form to treat it, the perturbation calculus, that only can go on sequentially from an adjustment to another of the successive bodies, or to draw up a surrounding approach for the limits of general resolution of the problem. Of a significantly analogous way for Samkhya, mind, that is sequential in its own nature and it cannot perceive two things simultaneously, is with more reason incapable to contemplate simultaneously the distinctive character of *gunas*; in fact mind cannot perceive itself directly, so it can perceive itself or *gunas* by inference, received knowledge or impression of consciousness that has no memory.

§ 7 §

Sattwa, *Rajas* and *Tamas* are, in their primary form, sensitivity, activity and inertia. Or, if we prefer, (relative) balance, mutability and potentiality. It is worth to notice that some circumstantial divisions such as *Grahita, Grahya* and *Grahana*, or the knower, the knowable and the means of knowledge, are not equally primary, because they are not exclusively referred to the conditioned nature, since we can understand the knower ambiguously either like *Purusha* or pure awareness, either like the intellect of an empirical subject that belongs to a material modality, *Sattwa* in this case.

On the matter of mind, we can say that it is not an exclusive attribute of *Sattwa* or the sensitivity, but that mind itself, although more clearly manifested in the state of *Sattwa*, contains mutability and inertia like inherently associated qualities. *The three* gunas *are included and present in any object or subject that we could separate: therefore the* gunas *or primary qualities are those that cannot be separate or isolate in any way, except by the momentary or relative dominion that one of the three always exerts on the*

[28]

others. In fact, if we considered the gear of the three like an internal or proper clock "isolated" from any other, we would reach by definition to the conclusion that does not exist any event or moment if some alteration or mutation between *gunas* has not taken place, no matter the slight this could be. *Gunas* themselves are temporary propensities and the changes of their disposition mark the "internal clock" or the proper time of the entities and processes. This does not happen because the entities could be isolated from environment in any special way, which is not the case, but simply by the fact that the change in anyone of the three qualities only can be detected in relation to the others.

§ 8 §

Then, we could get a clock for proper time. Let us remember that the inertia principle of Galileo leads, in the interpretation of the correlative motion between systems, to the principle of Galilean relativity that tell us that no system can measure its motion from itself, but in relation to external others. The later theories of relativity, special and general, are extensions of the same case taking the speed of light as reference. We continued counting the time with an absolute clock like the Newtonian one because we are incapable to find a clock of proper or internal time. The quantum theory of radiation and matter does not change this because it is postulated like invariant with respect to the time, the space and the direction. Peculiarly, often it is said that their events do not depend on the absolute time, only trying to mean that they do not depend on a "before" or a "later" within the universal synchronous time. In fact, such invariants are postulated to maintain the principles of conservation of energy and moment, in last instance dependents of the inertia principle, facilitating therefore the calculations. Certainly, there is not another way, because even if variations were detected, *it does not exist any other clock* to measure them or to compare them. They would be always random events, which always will have a place in the barely outlined frame of probability

[29]

amplitude. What is decisive here is that within the frame of the mechanics *it does not fit nor can conceive another clock: if we could have it, we would not know what to measure with it.* The Universal, Global Synchronization Clock ,always forces to us to measure the things in relation to external events, appealing if necessary to the Zero Time and the Big Bang itself as the release of the spring; but it is not possible another idea of the clock from this perspective, the clock is already the perfect and absolute synchrony of the events –an apparent a priori that nevertheless is derived from the inertia principle and its ideal plane. In the sense of the global or universal synchronization, the key of every other, it is not true at all that the theory of relativity has overflowed the kantian frame, because it has not overflowed the one of Newton nor the one of Galileo either; the fundamental statement has not changed and it has been merely enriched with contents. The same is valid, although not in the same proportion, for the quantum mechanics.

§ 9 §

It works in the same way when we consider the so called "internal clocks", for which Biology is the privileged field. Such clocks, now molecules now groups of cells, do not play another role that this one of synchronize itself to each other and altogether to synchronize themselves with the outside. ADN itself is a timer with very delicate dependencies in its modulation. Of course, pieces for this mechanism exist, and they must exist; the question is where the knot of its correspondence is. In other words, we have to know if there is a mechanism in addition to the pieces. As both things are assumed, the "mechanism" must be synchronous with the exterior, and this is already what defines the mechanisms in the way we have used to understand them. From this point of view with no possible escape, it is absolutely inconceivable that something not mechanical could exist, and the only that make some differences are the degrees of determinism and predictability. For that reason any variety of biological determinism has already given a form

[30]

in which it must fit materials and data; this form is not so much any content of chemistry or physics, for example, but the forced reference to the outside without specifics breaks of continuity.

§ 10 §

Gunas or primary properties of the Samkhya, as the last discernible by the intellect, and only if it becomes present to the awareness, would only have to be the objective par excellence, and this is precisely why, whereas immediate knowledge, is absolutely unattainable for any attempt of direct measurement. This is excluded by definition: whoever that want to perceive directly *gunas*, already knows what must do. For that Patanjali wrote the *Yoga-sutras*. To perceive differently *gunas* implies already to perceive them free, free of all mixture, and therefore, immovable – not nonexistent, but incapable to manifest anything. To this we can refer the state of *Kaivalia*, the state free of qualities and released from the bonds. As the bonds are *gunas* for themselves, the state of *Kaivalia* or exemption can be preached with so much more property of the conditioned nature that of the same consciousness, that already is postulated like unaffected. If the identity that underlies in this is denied in a separation gesture, is for avoiding the same compulsion of identity like synonymous of the confusion that is worth to avoid; beyond this extreme consequence there is not the least reason to consider the Samkhya like a dualist system. The more we could say is that, if liberation exists, in that liberation the same nature concurs. This would have been a maximum motif for the philosophy if the theology and the dogma would not buried it.

§ 11 §

Returning to the subject of the measurability of *gunas*, since they are only exempt at the moment of their cessation, it could be assume that they have some sort of mixture or confusion while they

[31]

exist fluctuating, or simply exist. But this it is a very delicate point since the own nature of *gunas* is the distinction, and in addition that distinction is the constituent of the moments in a "proper time" that does not need an external reference. Therefore, it is always preferable to speak of an interaction, marked always by the dominion of one of the qualities over the other two. It could be asked if this interaction is temporary or strictly simultaneous, that is to say, if the reconfigurations of *gunas* obey to a causal struggle between them which entails an internal time, or if they are reshaped without a factor of time in pure simultaneity without internal cause at all, that in any case would be necessary to look for outwards. It is easy to see that this takes to a new version of the everlasting antinomies of motion, the continuity, the time and others. Since we do not try to find solution them with the mere thought, we have to look for experimental models with formal validity also, that is to say, adapted to our methods of measurement. The possibility of such methods was the departure question, that is to say, how to measure what it assumes immediate. The definitive answer that can give the Samkhya to us agrees in this with the one the Vedanta, the classical non-dualism could give: it does not exist nor it can exist a last and irreducible difference between mediate and the immediate things, continuous and the discontinuous things, the motion and the rest or the interior and the exterior. We could not speak about anything if such things could exist, and if we did not speak, hardly they would exist more.

Therefore, the less than we can do is to leave us by the tangent of similar conventions created by and for the thought, and to see what the tangent draws between the real things and the term of cease of thoughts. Which will be constituted as well by new thoughts, now perhaps guided by a better understanding and fortune.

§ 12 §

Samkhya conceived a purely empirical science that hardly could have some value for the eyes of the moderns. It was *the Ayurveda*, the science of the care of the life, not very distant in the spirit of other old medical arts, like the hippocratic medicine or the Chinese one. What distinguishes the ayurvedic frame in its humoral theory is to be an application or contemplation of the frame of *gunas*. Three humors or *doshas*, *vata*, *pitta* and *kapha*, or wind, bile and phlegm, are not but reactive forms of the inherent properties of sentience, activity and inertia. By reactive it has to be understood that its predominance on the other properties is able to generate imbalances and ailments throughout the time; but also that they are secondary or derived form from more original and less privative modalities in the constitution of the subject: *prana, tejas* and *ojas*, the vital breath, the brilliance of the combustion and the radical oil that pervades and nourish the body. Now we treat with a much more material qualification of *gunas*, but exactly in the same way subject to the same fundamental logic.

It has been noticed sufficiently by the scholars the influence of the ayurvedic concepts in authors like Plato, in *Thimeus* particularly, where he wrote openly about the "air, phlegm and the bile", besides to mention "the established periods of life... in conformity with the triangles of the nature of each one" .It is really peculiar to observe how this book of mysteric root and pole of the enlightened hermetic philosophy has provided a rational inspiration for varied readers of scientific die, from Kepler and Galileo to Heisenberg. Another one of the platonic divisions of the soul in vegetative, sensitive and rational, is also of net Indian origin, or in any case it at least and admits a strictly congruent superposition with *kapha, pitta* and *vata*, and the corresponding functions of vegetative plasticity, irritability, and sensitivity.

Even the traditional contemplation of the man like body, soul and spirit keeps a strict correspondence, if not in extension or expression, yes in the most intimate nature of its correlations; being this consideration the only thing that matters. We will not mention the numerous triads of identical nature that the reader can easily imagine.

§ 13 §

In the beginning, any attempt to define better *gunas* or the correspondent *doshas* exhausts in mere epithets and paraphrases. We can use some semantic approaches, but trying to grant to the semantics the minimum of respect that deserves. After all, our investigation can take us to the conclusion that it does not exist a way to eliminate the "semantic questions", and not in last instance but throughout all its formulation, since we would be trying to show in a convincing and useful way the non-separation principle or property.

The three *gunas* also can comfortably be classified like centripetal, centrifugal and orbiting propensities. In respect to the *doshas*, that aspect relatively more material of the primary qualities, *pitta* makes reference to the heat and the energy, *kapha* to the plasticity and solidity, *vata* to all the phenomena of circulation from which the form is derived –of the more isolable or pure aspect of form insofar as independent of the plastic and the dynamic moments. It could be objected that this last one is a mere entelechy; we will try to see that it is not so simple.

Contemplating a tree we can see and touch characteristics such as colour, forms and texture. To say that the intrinsic combination of those external characteristics is the result or the appearance of primary qualities like the growth, condensation and formation can sound too unspecific and arbitrary. But if we would burn the tree, we could distinguish perfectly between something that actually burns, something that is reduced to ashes, and something that rejects both things and is freed in the form of steam and smoke. *The form* is what it evaporates and disappears, speaking in the

[34]

superficial sense or in the deepest. Steam and smoke not is simply the result of that which burns, but very contrary is what escapes of burning, as well as, on the other hand, escapes momentarily from the gravity. Although the scrutiny of this can take much more far, is sufficient to make see that, of the most violent form, while these qualities still maintain some relation to each other, they have unmistakable behaviours. The form is not absolutely an abstraction, unless we could understand by "abstraction" the very distillation or circulation made by the same tree and nature itself.

§ 14 §

Within this ayurvedic frame of *doshas*, there exists a clinical procedure par excellence: *nadi vigyan*, the auscultation of the pulse. Those who practice it with unequal fortune are often called vadyas, seers or performers, according to the literal translation. The auscultator successively feels the radial artery of the subject with the three middle fingers of the hand, alternating the pressure, in an analogous way as playing a string or wind instrument. The auscultation becomes after a sufficient interval of rest.

The separated or "independent" characteristics of the pulse are recognized from always like five: rhythm or rate, frequency, intensity, amplitude and form.

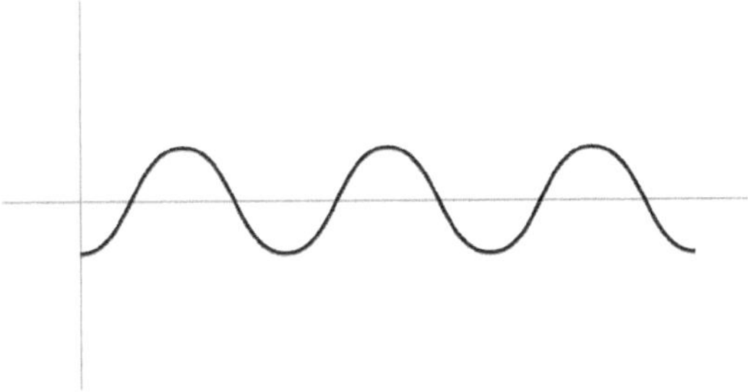

Fig. 1

We have now a biological oscillator. We can perfectly understand the first four of them in the analytical sense of an oscillator. The basic frequency is the number of beats or cycles in a sufficient period of time, a minute, for example. The rate or rhythm is the measurement of the regularity or irregularity of the cycles throughout the greater period. The intensity is the peak altitude reached about the tops of the wave of the pulse. Finally, the amplitude registers the total difference between those maximums and the minimums of the bottom or valley of the wave. Of these four, the obtained frequency is constituted apparently in rigid base for the possible variations of the others: the rate or regularity not only affects to the relations between cycles, also it is necessary to consider the compression or stretching of their own duration. The intensity as the amplitude can be variable also, based on the pathologies. The basic frequency can be considered rather rigid because in normal conditions the variations of the other elements would not have to relapse into it; but in a more comprehensive plane also the frequency is determined by the others. In addition to these four elements that we can treat analytically, we have *the form* of the pulse. During a long time, the mechanical sphygmographs or pulse-graphs could not detect with sufficient acuity this true and evasive *quinta essentia*; it has been necessary to wait to the small laser diodes and other technologies to catch his profile suitably. These technologies do not register anything essentially different from that which an expert auscultator catches with its fingers, the only thing that do is to shape them graphically and to offer them as a challenge to the analysis.

Is the form of the pulse a strict result of the other four analytical components, or contains something irreducible? But we have still not specified what we have to understand in the pulse as *form*. The form is not only the set of variations of height inside the phase or cycle,

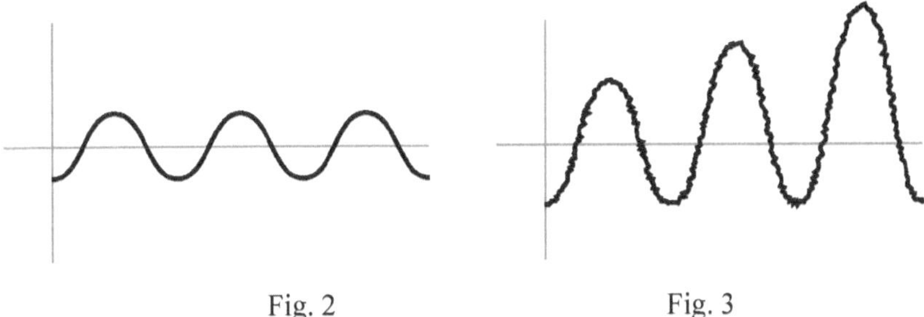

Fig. 2   Fig. 3

as it is appraised in figure 3 with respect to figure 2; it also incorporates in itself the thickness of the feature as a whole, that can be more or less homogenous, or to have very important differences (Figures 4, 5 and 6),

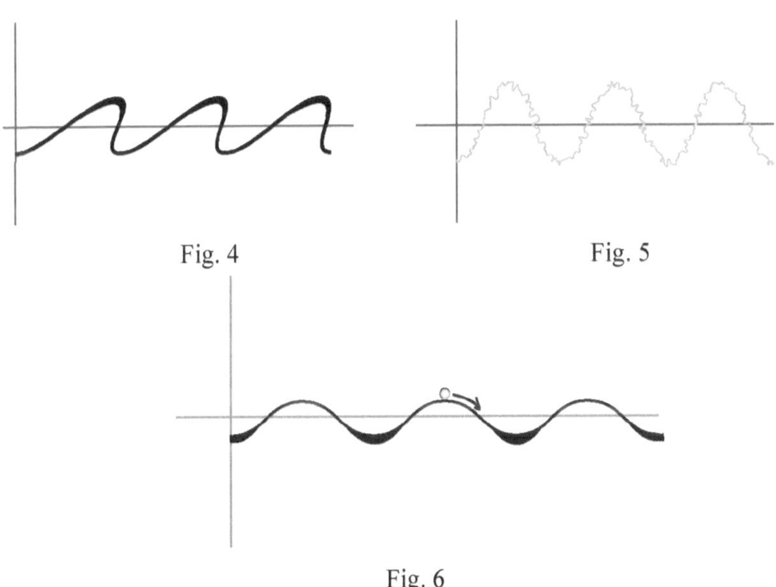

Fig. 4   Fig. 5

Fig. 6

either comparatively among them, or inside each cycle for the same pulse, or, even, between different pulsations or beats from a same auscultation, that would be resulting of a great imbalance or of an internal or external removal. The Chinese pulsology, in

[37]

essential agreement with India, has characterized with epithets such as "silk worm having nibbled a mulberry leaf", or "small ball sliding in a porcelain cup" to pulses similar to those of figures 5 and 6. It is easy to understand that such shades have escaped for a long time to mechanical detectors. Now that problem no longer exists and all this can be caught by minimum devices; in addition, in this way all type of dynamic sequences in motion situations or effort can be obtained, something impossible in the traditional procedure. The changes of the ambient temperature also introduce revealing modifications. To this another treatment of great interest can be superposed, the sound recording and its harmonic analysis. Not we forget that the main meaning of word *nadi* is channel or hollow tube, and that in the Hindu conception is the relative "vacuum" what resonates, more than what is filling it. But we return again to the subject of the form.

It is evident that this form of pulse recording, considered separately, admits an analytical treatment, since the reader connected to the detector is integrating the results according to the rate of the samples; on the other hand, also the thickness of the plot or feature admits a differential by its own fluctuation in time. But here finishes all the similarity: what we cannot integrate is the five characteristics with its different ranks of variations in a formula simpler that the obtained reading pulse itself. For that reason it is a non-analytical system. This seems to be largely studied by the different forms of modern cardiography, which is experiencing an extraordinary development now. It is indeed by this technological development, and, peculiarly, by the non-analytical character of the data, that the cardiology and the medicine of the biomedical model ignore completely, or at least as much as it is possible, the intrinsically semiotic character of the pulse in the traditional conception. That is to say, being a signal not of analytical character, experts tend to fit in it everything what effectively is possible to analyze or, at least, to separate in parts, which results more in the detailed pursuit of the implied corporal structures. However, well understood, this motion would not be absolutely in opposition to the traditional posing, which matters very little that pulse as "system" is not analytical, since, on the contrary, which looks for in it is *the more irreducible signature and the more able to synthesize the rest of the data, known or to be know.* One assumes that the profile of the pulse is the result, definitive and unquestionable, in the same way that in the stock market, the market of the speculation, the same speculations in the whole possible set of orders and powers always refers to the present or current value –indeed, the reason of speaking about "to take the pulse" to the market.

Is to be present that also the three *doshas* or implied reactive humours in the pulse can easily be separate in three factors or precise mechanical moments: in most general of the terms *pitta* corresponds with the contractile impulse of the heart, *vata* with the state of the walls of the vessel and its own conduction of the contractile wave, *kapha* with the fluidity or viscosity of the blood. Even like independent terms of a problem of mechanics of fluids, these three factors already are sufficient to create a non-linear system without stable values in the solutions; but in fact what happen is that there is an intrinsic dependency and feedback among them. Still more, the great relative stability that only throws the results can be conceived by its mutual reaction, which often is denominated, with unlucky term, *self-organization.* To understand to what extent is not necessary that "self-organization", is to go further on as much of the mechanics as of the theory of the ignorance that we call complexity theory.

§ 15 §

About the comprehensive and predictive value of the coordinates of *tridosha* in the medical exercise of the diagnosis and the prognosis, the subject is too open for hasty conclusions, ignoring those who consider such marks as empirical rudiments or even superstitions. And it is opened by several fronts and reasons. First of all, we can be sure that in this medical art, like in any other,

[39]

are many those that practice it and well few those that have some mastery over it. But it is not enough to say that the subject is as vast as the same health or the life, that is difficult and complicated. It could be really, specially if it is lacked necessary sensitivity, or of the necessary education of sensitivity. Certainly the term complexity deserves often an indicated parenthesis. Operations and the diverse manipulations could be "difficult" or "complicated"; listening or the understanding does not try to thread or to untie the knots, but to follow them in which they can give of themselves.

Although these deficiencies of sensitivity that all we suffer do not have quick solution, still turns out more devilish paradoxical to want to solve the subject giving it parameters. We can, is certain, to assign values or relative weights to the three *doshas*; but this only has an approaching value, to which it is not possible to give a scale very fit scale of precision. Nobody, that we could know, has measured the relative weight of the three tendencies in centesimal values, which even seems absurd, unless we were filling up a test by points. Not even we know if there is a degree of relevant precision, aside from more fundamental questions like the nature and sequence of the reactions. Soon we warn ourselves of the unnatural thing that is to want to turn a procedure into a method. By very valid this could be, it must be recognized that was not developed thinking about numbers, even if samkhya means *number*. And nevertheless, the nucleus or subject of all this continues being something as simple as the proportion and the balance: and not of an immensity of factors, but only three...

We can return to ask to us if the pulse really contains as much information or if it is not rather an illustration of the knowledge acquired by the doctor with other symptoms. But it is not so; it is more probable that the aspect of a patient could be illustrative of the pulse that in the contrary way, if the doctor has enough aptitude; although both enrich and complement the judgment. On the other hand we can also try to reframe to us if the frame of the three tendencies is really necessary and sufficient. Naturally, *vadya* will say yes to us, and the only thing that we can do it is to accept or not to accept his rules of game. After all, for Samkhya the only form to verify if *gunas* exists or not is following them until the end. Samkhya is the procedure of that verification, not a theory or method.

§ 16 §

Then it will be necessary to make use of our immense arsenal of applied mathematics to headless problems. An ideal candidate would be the fuzzy logic and its sets. Ideal, because the very high grades of precision do not seem pertinent; in addition, the fuzzy logic is a suitable treatment for control systems and expert systems. Both things is what represents the pulse if is considered alternatively it from within and from outside.

In order to create an expert system we must transfer the knowledge of the expert, in this case the *vadya*, turning it into quantitative estimations and rules of inference. It will be needed a minimum several hundreds of samples, that can ascend to a thousand or several thousands. The estimation of the proportions of the agents or tendencies becomes as precise as it seems opportune for the *vadya*. In no case such estimations for the input of data will be of a very high precision; probably a scale from 0 to 10, or perhaps only from 0 to 6. For example, 4 of *kapha*, 1 of *vata* and 1 of *pitta*. Which already is telling us that such estimation is more than nothing indicative and that what matters in this case is the dominant one. There could occur cases without dominant too (a third of each one), and those pulses will be most regular and less not-linear. If this scale of entrance is not even very precise, the sum of cases and its averages by the expert system would tend in the long run to increase too much the precision, if this one really were relevant. It could move perhaps in a rank of hundredth, or thousandth even. Have we gained something with this? Are not we deforming the original data yet? To this it is necessary to say that the expert person, in the first place, *does not realize everything*

[41]

what he knows. That is to say, that his knowledge is not explicit except in a small degree that permit him to communicate, to learn and to teach. Surely he has not thought at all about quantitative or numerical terms, and he will continue without needing it. His sensitivity gives another kind of data to him, and among them, a very important one: the tendency within the tendency.

§ 17 §

The *Vadya* discern between *prakriti* and *vikriti*, the biological and the biographical thing, the original or innate constitution of individual and its tendencies acquired throughout the life. By definition, any later state in the health of the subject is dependent and it is refer to the constitutional tendencies; so that the habits or alterations produced in the meantime are, on one hand, already assimilations of the eventualities to an original conformation, and, on the other hand, that same conformation that has its slopes of reaction respect to the accidental conditions or *vikriti*. If *prakriti* and *vikriti* come to be like substance and accidents for a given pulse, for that reason it is not necessary to forget that in the long run those accidents or way of life can get to be most decisive for the conservation or destruction of the balance that represents the health. But not in vain it is spoken then about the way of life as the specific form of life. In an essential way, the form only is modified by its own form of wind itself in time, and that thread has to be perceived by *vadya* with right sensitivity.

However we consider it, it does not stop being an extraordinary wonder the fact of that fundamental persistence of the form of the pulse throughout all a life, if we think about the immense variety of circumstances that can surround it and alter it, and how slight is its signal. If we think about that this little thread of time is going to maintain something of its own in the most adverse circumstances, beyond the successive losses of identity of the memory, and that not even a violent death can rob the right to him to disappear according to its own and intimate law.

[42]

§ 18 §

This distinction of the tendency within a tendency is so fundamental for our study as it was it the distinction between speed and acceleration for the birth of dynamics through the concept of force. The hydrodynamic systems or fluids mechanics -a circuit of pipes with water to pressure- cannot establish this type of differences because the components are not connected from the origin, and all the differentials we could measure later depend on the arbitrary variation of parameters. A primary and original reference does not exist. It is well known on the other hand the dependency or sensitivity of the not-linear systems with respect to the initial data, considered here in another order. Therefore, the initial vagueness that results from the qualitative study of the pulse also has a very important counterpart that is unthinkable in the traditional analysis. Only by this already would be worth to study thorough *nadi vigyan*. But it is that in addition this original qualification to *doshas* would have to give us the key to measure that *proper time* of beings and the entities that is not possible to conceive in the analytic frame.

In another order of things, and ignoring which could be its relation, it is worth to remember that still it is object of discussion, study and modelling the problem of the forms of flow of the sanguineous torrent. It is conjectured if this flow, that of course is not laminate but with very varied turbulences, can follow helical or spiral guidelines, which doubtless would optimize its diffusion. I am convinced of the rightness of this hypothesis, and is surprising in any case that such elemental unknown factors would persist for processes in our immediate interior and within canals of millimeters or centimeters of span, when it has been possible to determine with great precision particle interactions in distances fifteenth magnitude orders smaller. This gives us a certain idea of the existing abyss in the analysis for different disciplines. And we can remember that until the year 2000 has not been generally recognized that the fibers of the heart form a spiral, a helix that simply stretches and it shrinks. And in the meantime there have been thousand and thousands of open-heart surgeries, and almost five centuries of detailed anatomy.

§ 19 §

Then, it is worth to give values to the *doshas* like fuzzy sets capable of relation. The expert system will be able to adjust more those values thanks to the average from many samples as well as thanks to the inferences that we allow him to generate. There are also simple rules of inference and others of superior orders. A simple one is, we take as example, "if the intensity increases, *pitta* also". The quantitative correlations by diverse means can settle down soon. More complex it would be: "if the intensity increases but the frequency diminishes...", etcetera. It is a simple work of exhausting, of exhaustion of the real possibilities. Anyway, the canonical classification of the fundamental pulses in twenty-odd types already facilitates sensibly the ordering of the criteria search. One of the advantages of the fuzzy expert systems is that they allow to make finite the number of inference rules to use, which is not the case for other models of probability. To make them finite is still far from making always the number of rules necessary to cover any system manageable, but it is no doubt that for a low not-linear system as this one there are no great difficulties of principle. The fuzzy or diffuse logic often has been erased to be simple logic of probabilities disguised. This can seem certain if it is wanted to see from outside, but the case is that the traditional logic of probabilities in its different variants cannot make finite its rules for the great majority of problems, so something important can be out of them. In other time, J. M. Keynes, the famous economist, tried to accede without success to an suitable formulation of the principle of "variety of limited logical independence", that at least was proposed. Today we see that this is impossible and inadmissible for the general context of the analysis, virtually infinitesimal. Nevertheless, that to which Keynes talks about in his approach to

[44]

the logic of the induction is something so reasonable because the limited cases cannot depend on a limitless number of rules. But so that this happens, rules are needed that are not perfectly analytical, that is to say, different rules that often occupy such cases in the same space of probability. In fact, the logic either is vague from the beginning, and crucial depends on the fortune of the applications that this is being notice later or earlier. The fuzzy logic turns over that deficiency as far as possible and can determine the weight of the redundancy of different rules. One of the initial theorems of the fuzzy logic demonstrates that the set of the real solutions is minor than its possible, statistical parts; this way is necessary to begin, since for the traditional probability the set is the sum of the whole separated possibilities.

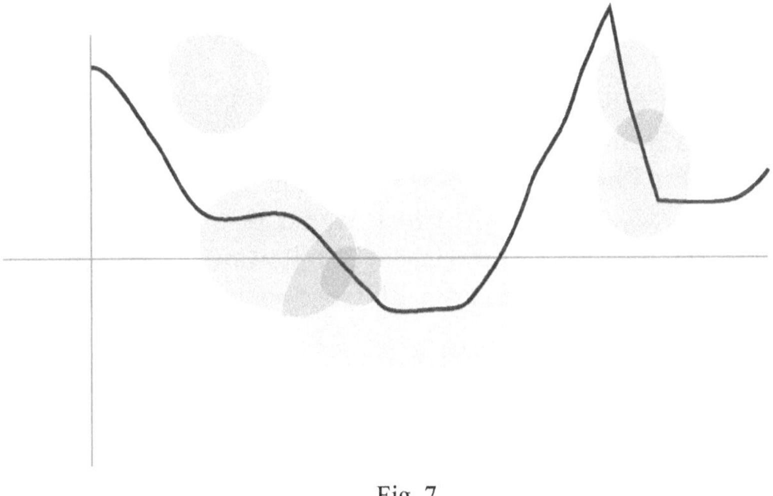

Fig. 7

§ 20 §

"The weight of the redundancy of different rules" is not but the fact that a position is confirmed from different angles or for different reasons; this over-determination is the counterpart of internal precision to the external imprecision that offers the fuzzy logic in its rules and values. One begins to suspect that this logic is not a mere approach of force to a problem that we ignored, but that even can help us to conceive that paradoxical "precision of the lack of definition" that with so mastery and indifference exhibits nature. This that we see like mere redundancy in the space of probability occupation, can be authentic over-determinacy in the "internal space" of the system or process, or better, in its "internal time", and to say it definitively, in its *proper time*.

Thus, at least, we could begin to conceive something that as a start and coming from the analysis seemed to us inconceivable.

§ 21 §

Being *gunas* authentic and genuine modalities, it is possible to ask ourselves about their relation with the modal logic, the logic of possibility, necessity and contingency. But these are so vast categories or modes that it turns out pretentious to speak of this logic like a real formal science. Surely, insofar as can follow the nature, it could be refined and be outlined in the Samkhya, instead of trying to give form to it, which would be absurd and in last instance impossible. The modal logic follows the modes, so the modes exist more than the modal logic. This justifies it and gives the limits to it.

§ 22 §

We return to the question of why such a simple and slight signature as this one of the pulse is able to represent so much variety of information. Only if the time has its own density, that is to say, if it admits different densities and thicknesses, we can know of what is reduction which we are perceiving like limit. The same signal already is the perfectly fit limit, inverting the perspective of the analysis. What before we called *form* of the pulse, as much in its particularity as in its surrounding, is as much the form of the limit and its formation.

[46]

§ 23 §

The monitoring of the temporary evolution of the pulse in dynamic sequences, that is to say, during the motion of the subject in situations of action and passion, of pleasure and pain, allows the extension of the reference field that the three *gunas* constitutes. Since *Tamas* already is the inert receiver the passions, *Rajas* is the removal by the action of the pain that as passion is its means, and *Sattwa* is the relative safe-placing as much of the pain as the action, which altogether we consider as pleasure. This way we can catch to what extent biological and the biographical thing, *prakriti* and *vikriti*, are not heterogeneous, but mutually continued. This would not be possible if the *gunas*, in any given constitution, did not incorporate in themselves their relation with the environment, of which the temporary evolution already is explanation, untacklement. In the total unity of measurement and mediation it resides all the excellence and the apparent difficulty of this procedure.

§ 24 §

Making use of this principle of over-determination or superimposition of the space occupied by the inferences, that refers to the weight of the things and to its cause in the sense of sufficient reason, we could verify that the same system or its equivalent graph tends to open, to close and to transpose spaces, or what is equal, it gives back guidelines of induction, deduction and hypothesis to us that we can try to complete in case the relation between values of the parameters and rules of inference has become stabilized or converged. Soon it can be judged to what extent and of what specific ways the system is breaking the moulds of the differential equations that we attributed to it. This has fundamental relations not only with algorithms and the study of the steps to describe a problem, but also with the economy of operations of the knowledge in general, and its composibility. If we can describe sufficiently a process without using differentials equations and analytical terms, nor there is an analytical form to decide which is the minimum sequence of inferences or its order. Although we handle with someone always.

§ 25 §

This seems inconceivable; more inconceivable than any principle of uncertainty. The smoothing of the roughness or complexity of a problem, of the joint of a function, seems to depend on an optimal order in the sequence; but that minimum requires for its definition a maximum of super- determination, of superior modes. But these also tends to yield and to be fused if they are really contained in the profile or *fit* form of the function. Now it can see that we are playing with a parallelism between the "expert system" and the "control system", between the cognitive approach and the natural process, as if they concurred in an identity. Both are needed for "working", although its independence is presupposed. Samkhya affirms that no absolute limit for the knowledge as for the perception does exist. Also affirms that all the set of the thought or knowledge subject to thought is, whereas mediated, least in relation to the being or the consciousness. If, following with the same logic, we wanted to try to understand how the paradox on the dimension of the knowledge is possible, its non-decidable compressibility or non- compressibility, we would also have to ask if the nature, the conscience, or being, is with respect to us an "expert system" or a "control system".

§ 26 §

But we return to the small things. If the pulse itself is one precise waterline for the set of the activities of a greater system, the body, manifested or not, we would have to be able to detect its temporary correlation with other subsystems. This correlation

[48]

does not have why to be very direct since the pulse would be a luck of indefinite integral with respect to the rest; the pulse would be a diffuse and fuzzy set in the other systems, and vice versa. In addition, the signals that other systems offer us not always give specific curves of the same type than the pulse. In this respect we must remember that for the medical technology and clinical all these indicators, whereas signals, are considered as *non specific*, in the sense that they are not sufficiently revealing of the functions, structures and mechanisms; from our point of view, we considered *specific* everything what he is inherently revealing of *gunas* or *doshas*, that is to say, what it express with sufficiency the modes.

The electrical signals, like that of electroencephalogram or the galvanic resistance of the skin, are less directly expressive than those purely mechanical of the pulse or the one of a neumograph adapted for the breathing. In electroencephalogram, for example, it would be necessary to add different frequencies or simultaneous amplitude to obtain equivalent from the thickness of the signature in the form of the wave, being blurred perhaps the form of the phase. This offers interesting questions of conversion of signals which now we cannot treat, related to the same nucleus of the quantum mechanics. In any case, in this type of measures we are far from the uncertainty threshold.

Finally, electrical or mechanical pulsating and oscillating rates cross the different systems until arriving at the same cells and their division. The important thing is in what degree we can catch the integral phenomenon of the form with the sufficiency that we found in the pulse. Then if there is something able to connect all these oscillators heterogeneous in many ways, that something is the form.

§ 27 §

The fuzzy logic has contributed to us something more than instruments at the time of finding the relevant qualities of the pulse; it has also give us a way to glimpse to what extent the nature can act independently of all our analytical logic and our equations, increasing on the contrary the thickness of his internal or own consistency. This already is much, and is possible to ask why the subject has not been investigated with more zeal. Perhaps the method is too strange to our concepts of formalization, and its apparent procedure towards the dark by darkest can produce terror. And nevertheless, many systems can adjust this way with a maximum economy.

Speaking about the form we have arrived at layers more and more unformed; and this could be the best signal that we have obtained a more real approach to the nature. But this absence of form disgusts and moves away to the mathematician, the only people who could help us here. They need an acceptable link to cross to this side.

Irremediably Galileo comes to the memory. It is well known that in the famous experiments with inclined planes he had to resort to the beats of his own pulsation like measurement of the time, in absence of a better one. To make matters worse, when he began to study the oscillators by means of improved and primitive pendulums, he could not arrive more far by the tragicomic circumstance that he needed a good pendulum clock to measure the time intervals accurately.

As for the rest, our modern notion of the oscillator does not go beyond knowing how round is a circle. One does not know what circulates because the reestablishment of the symmetry and the balance are already assumed. Even when it is spoken of a symmetry rupture is for justifying the supposed symmetry, that already it is given, outside there . It is not to be strange then that seems to us strange the notion of many cultures of a circular time. Why they want to go nowhere with as much delivery? When it is so easy to go outside there, where already is everything. And giving rounds, in addition.

But it is not difficult to see that the only thing that moves is the imbalance, and that is the balance the precarious, problematic and the delicate thing. Seeing thus, the science of dynamics could treat more on any thing than on the motion.

Very little of this is rhetorical if we return to the unavoidable surprise and difficulty that a simple phenomenon as pulse according to our exposition provokes. It is necessary to see first the range of our ignorance when we spoke of "self-organization". We do not really understand that although nature would like to organize itself in its free moments, it results that it has not free moments because we have already given to it a permanent and full time occupation in the space of dynamics. Still we even look for new spaces and places to work more! An infinity of spaces, without the smaller temporary density. And that this is a real problem for the analysis, is evidenced in the fact that the more recent theoretical physics, after its extraordinary deployment in eleven dimensions, still has had to resort to objects of dimension zero and non-commutative geometry in which a point no longer is a point but all a matrix of possible values, discountable values, we suppose. It seems that we want to catch something already excluded in the definition. Our strange means of inference, however, have been nets to give a form to that without form, more than to capture this slippery and mysterious fish. Leaving this preliminary squids fishing apart, it would be very easy to say that we are treating completely different problems, but we do not believe it. No analysis worth of this name tolerates completely different problems.

§ 28 §

Everything would be simpler if our measurement of the time were already a measurement of the asymmetry. But we can ask if such thing exists and in what respect. Modern cosmology already parts of events of balance rupture, from which data and observable things would be the result. We, on the contrary, and without

[51]

opposition spirit, give by fact that are the imbalances those that exist from always and those that want to be perpetuated always, which could not be for a moment nor without pacts with the balance or even series of pacts, that constitute them and maintain. As much the act to persist in its being as the one to agree to the balance necessities falls under the concept of reaction of *gunas*, and surely is impossible to discern if in last instance they are not identical.

But we need some departure point or reference. The physics uses rigid, external and absolute values of reference: the speed of light, the action quantum, the intensity of gravity. Other absolutely necessary values of reference exist, such as the specific weight of the vacuum and its relation with the observed minimum masses, those of different particles; but in this case no longer we can know if there are rigid values, neither external, nor absolute. In any case the previous constants give us the meter and the clock with which to measure and to compare all type of events and things no matter how different they were. In the same way which we ignored the relation of these three constants with the indefinite fields of reference, we cannot either know if these three constants are so at least congruous, that is to say, if they have some real possibility at least to converge; as we either do not know in the other hand if the duration, the mass and the distance are homogenous or non-homogeneous properties to each other, or in other words, if its relation can be closed and be defined lawfully in its own terms without another external reference. Such case, the external would have become internal and we could enjoy a lasting transparency. But I suppose that no physicist tries to take the things so far.

Our reference point can be neither rigid, nor absolute, nor external. Nor internal at least. It must be proportional, be based intrinsically on the proportionality. But the proportion is based on a meter or scale, is said.

§ 29 §

Often the things show us their own proportions. For example, the average distances between the successive bifurcations in the branches of a tree, or in the sequence of lengths of our same members; those proportions do not require an external reference, since they are independent of the meter whereupon we measure them. We even can compare between them the specific proportions of different examples of trees of a same species or different species, and they do not lose anything of his intrinsic character. For the analysis, all this accumulation of varied relations conforms the circumstantial, the descriptive thing, *the unspecific* of an object, even when could be the most significant for us. Since the analysis has convert the time into space without admitting appeal, the only worth to do in this case is to reveal the temporary element that there is behind these processes or developments that occupy a space. The "external" form of a tree is already the form of its development, in first plane and over any other consideration. That first plane surrounds to all the others. The form is not something secondary, adjective or circumstantial. In fact, it does not exist at all something like an isolated external form, exists an outer contour of which it is broken through, indeed, by the form of action, and that is intrinsically temporary, and therefore, neither internal. Time has nothing to do with the "inside" or the "outside".

§ 30 §

In the last decades of the XX century was developed an increasing interest between the mathematicians on the generative relations that proliferate around the *Phi* number (Φ), also known like Golden Mean or Golden Section, and other epithets. As it is well known, the golden mean is the relation given by the cut in a point C of the segment unit AB of such form that the smaller segment AC has a measurement with respect to the greater CB equal to which this one has with original segment AB

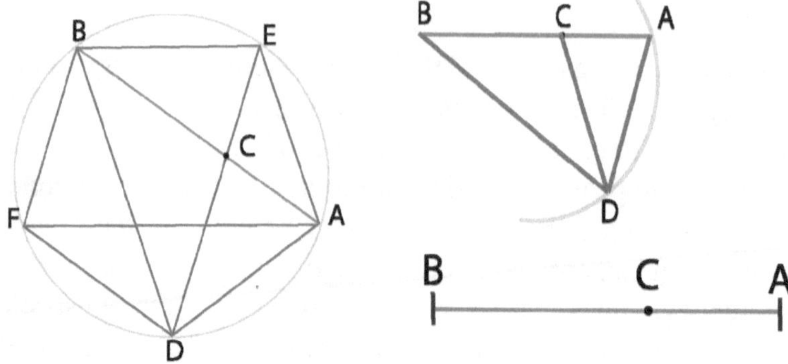

Fig. 8

The value of this relation can be expressed indifferently like 0.618... or 1.618... (1+V5)/2, according to if we fold or we unfold the segment towards the interior or the outside. This continuity of the inequality, or this discontinuity of the equality, as much by the operation as by the proportion, and as much towards the interior as towards the exterior of the indifferent unit of reference, is deserved of being considered like *the Continuous Proportion* par excellence, and thus we will call it onwards.

If we looked for proportions between the different measures from an object, as well as of the different reasons among them (being the same reason than proportion), the concatenation of those reasons and the reasons of reasons in indefinite number always would have to refer us to some approach to Φ like the simple possible reason. This, by definition. It is for that reason that the value of use of the Continuous Proportion and anyone of its approaches does not have in itself anything of arithmological -as somebody could believe-, inasmuch it always refers to the simplest reason. What is subject of doubt here, what is problematic is the application, the pertinence: but this one is the problem that defines *phi* itself, or rather, the reason of its application. If we remember the problem of over-determination in our previous sketch of the pulse like a fuzzy system, we can see that it is the same in essence. The Continuous

[54]

Proportion, *phi*, is as much the meter or the measurement as the set of the measurement modes. It is measurement and mediation in a single and same act, which give it the character in all the measures and of all the systems of measurement. It could only be alien to those systems of measurement that had demonstrated the internal self- determination of their constants, which would constitute his absolute character. At the moment, this is not the case for physics, and it would not be little know how to formulate the question of if this is possible in general. Or in other words, the whole exercise of physics is that question without its corresponding formulation.

§ 31 §

It has been said that the Golden Measurement is the top of a pyramid of which we do not know everything, since nothing we know of its height or its base. For Kepler, it was a treasure only comparable with the formulation of the Pythagorean theorem, that as well it is known was known and diversely demonstrated by other previous cultures. Also the Continuous Proportion, raised for annals by Euclides, could be well well-known by other cultures even if we only can conjecture on the matter. In any case it seems evident that the same Greeks knew it before Euclides, and, in fact, we can superpose the Pythagorean theorem and the Continuous Proportion in a same problem in one of his simpler expositions, and in simplest and equidistant of the problem of the equality and inequality, the mathematical rationality and the irrationality, that inaugurates all the possible slopes of thought. Thus it shows before us this Proportion its irreducible nature, its depth and its sublimity.

§ 32 §

We know inherently in which slope the Pythagorean theorem began to roll as a ball, by the same fact that all the fundamental concepts developed later, from the differential calculus to the

[55]

uncertainty principle, are refer in its irreducible form to the mentioned theorem. Thus, it is possible to contemplate in front of us the whole panorama of the Analysis. That we have forgotten almost completely that must exist another slope, the chance whispers maliciously to us that the mentioned theorem takes the name of a Greek philosopher and not the one of a Babylonian or Indian mathematician. It exists, in addition, the extremely remarkable fact that the innumerable developments that are receiving the Continuous Proportion and that unfold in all the imaginable directions are not mixed in minimum with the developments and key points of the Analysis, to which are not of any aid. Perhaps by this it has gotten to be spoken of his mutual complementariness, which actually means that mathematical of the Balance or the Harmony is complementary of the Analysis, whereas the Analysis is completely self- sufficient and it does not need complements.

This situation could change.

§ 33 §

Therefore, and for whom that knows to see it, the subtle winding of the thread of the Continuous Reason in the recent years offers a moving spectacle. Treating about the non-analytical thing, it is as much the product of the Analysis as what it is the vomited by it. Its empire is the nobody-land that grows everywhere between the different disciplines as these are branched off and diverged. But whereas Continuous Reason, has its own winding rhythm and familiar forms to which it does not resign whatever it is the treatment: like a brilliant living serpent appearing from a machine for sausages.

§ 34 §

Leonardo Pisano, Fibonacci, gave with the elementary sequence of numbers that tends with increasing exactitude to the irrational value of Φ: 1, 1, 2, 3, 5, 8, 13, 21, 34, 55, 89...The numbers are generated adding both previous terms, and the reason between adjacent terms give us the successive degrees of approach or precision. Fibonacci deduced the sequence as solution of two problems without the least apparent connection: that famous of the reproduction of a pair of rabbits in ideal conditions and the other, less known but equally revealing, of the optimal weights in a balance to make the smaller number of operations or manipulations. We can not to know until what conscience arrived him about the relation with the Continuous Proportion, as we either do not know the one that could have Al-Khwarizmi or Abu-Kamil, of whose problems extracted its wonderful generalization; but it is inevitable to see that only the development of the analysis could give to the subject its own relief and its contrast. And in effect, the generalized forms must mainly wait for until Binet and Lucas, until the development and maturity of the same concept of function.

Without its generative and self-recursive capacity of approach, *phi* would be to us of so little utility as the value of *pi* for a circle that does not admit the division in degrees; in both cases that intrinsic property makes possible algebraic generalizations and the elementary and superior functions. As on the other hand the connections of the Continuous Proportion with *pi* and *e*, the second subordinated constant of the analysis, is always weak and accidental, it has not been possible to arrive very far in the marriage between this one and what A. Stakhov has called, with enough justification, harmony mathematics.

Somebody said, with great sensible choice, that if we know to truss the framework for the relations between *pi, phi* and *épsilon*, in addition to its contacts with music and geometry in general, we would have reached the simplest and optimal understanding of the nature that within the formalisms we could dream. It is not a small program. *Epsilon*, the measurement of the non-linearity, in its varieties or constants, already constitutes in itself a sufficient labyrinth for anyone, and in any case it seems the knot that ties a whole package of problems, well closed for us. But it is to note that here nobody talks about the e constant. We amply know its essential paper in the analysis, their inherent character without question; soon is here a sovereign indication. The number e, synonymous of the compound interest and number of the accumulation par excellence, mirror of the proportionality in the functions, include in itself and like limit the series of all the fractions. Like exponential number, it reigns in the probabilistic space of the values and its products; and it is not necessary to say that almost all the values of the analysis already are products, result of the multiplication of factors. As well as the generativity is expressed through sum of terms and their limits, it is possible to say that the values product of a multiplication of terms already express a jump in the emptiness that is impossible to quantify from the result because it depends on the nature of those values. Let us think for example about the mass or the energy of a system, for which we do not know its natural units and we must be contented with equivalences, resultants as well of other products. The number e, like operator in the corresponding functions, has become to represent that necessary bridge between sum of terms and their products, but in decided please of these last ones, which are those that conform the elementary values. It is no wonder this expansion of empty spaces has provoked the maximum exigencies of rigor since Gauss and Cauchy. But in physics no rigor can affect the base of this process: he legitimacy of the conversion of sum in products will always depend on that exist pure units, unaffected and free of factors. To want to look for something thus in physics would be today inappropriate and absurd.

§ 36 §

And nevertheless, we remain feeling that in this way something very important is ignored or is harmed in the integrity of the processes, and the things. The statistical spaces, the measures of order or disorder, the entropy as logarithm of the probability, are only unquestionable in pure discreet mathematics; in *the real* world we only have correlations whose factors must be affected in last instance and necessarily. We can think about the three constants of the physics before alluded to, or in the three more fundamental magnitudes.

So that, not without audacity, we can venture that the unavoidable presence of the *e* number in the analysis is a good indicator of all that we attribute to chance and the ignorance in the real processes, whereas the presence of *phi* indicates perhaps an endless search of the generative sufficient reasons. The numbers *e* and *phi* would express antagonistic tendencies, more than complementary, although fortunately nothing prevents us to work whatever we want with both.

As much *pi* as *phi* are "highly natural" ratios, within the context of mathematical formalization, and could be known by different peoples from the antiquity. The number *e*, nevertheless, is an exclusive concept of the later Christian West. We do not know for how long will last its reign.

§ 37 §

With too much frequency one says that the man fears at chance, and that he try to take refuge from it with systems or theories. But in many aspects we need it so much as to breathe, and nothing would frighten so much to us as to suspect that the things

[59]

could be ordered until the last degree, and mainly if that last degree depended on us, who completely we ignored it. The chance is ignorance and the ignorance a positive support for our acts and also for the same knowledge. It is not conceivable that the chance could be in the existence, but for the existence, of which it is deduced that many have conceived little both existence and chance. Much more that the chance, to the man has worried to him and it would have to worry to him not to ignore or to be in opposition to the laws that make their existence possible, those laws or law which never is necessary to give form. The reasons that the Continuous Proportion looks for —or that resides in it—, even starting off very substantively of the form, lay for that direction, and in that same measure it can be save of the infinite search and the delirium. If we did not request too much the things are enough. The Analysis, with their emphasis in the precision or exactitude, is already the ideal frame to isolate the systems of their context, considered in form of strange influences to which it is wanted to consider. Even it surprises that this were not more fragile, if one forgets that this has been the means of its sensitivity.

§ 38 §

In the same way that the number e can generate all the frequencies, the Fourier transformation can "analyse" any package of waves in the resulting spectrum. Since it may be infinite different packages for each spectrum, but a single spectrum for each package, is evident that there is loss of information, in particular of the phase of the waves. The so call principle of non- determination or uncertainty is derived from these inherent limitations of the mathematical method, and is difficult to see why would have to be a general principle of nature. The same quantum of action is not simply an amount of work or energy per second, but per cycle/second, omission that tends to forget the phenomenon of frequency like evident, when it is all the opposite. By the same way we arrived at the superior generalizations of the gauge fields, that takes care

[60]

of conservations of symmetry –local or global-for the changes of phase, and not for the same phases, which in this context no longer seems to have any sense.

The space of waves of the physics, more synthetic than analytical, is basically a one dimension, linear and abstract space that admits the most ideal of the extrapolations to the ordinary dimension of the events. But —and this is the important thing here— that idealization does not have why to absolutely mean a simplification of the facts, but it also adds an imaginary complexity to them that would only occur in the case that waves did not have their proper binds and their own modes: those that on the other hand could not find place in the analysis, except by certain signatures and signs. That is to say, by nothing proper or specific. Here is the difficulty and the general incredulity when someone speaks of such hypothetical proper modes, that would have to be everywhere.

§ 39 §

In the meantime many theoreticians and dissident experimenters, or simply freer of commitments, give to tests with water in the bathtub or basic simulations in a computer. And certainly their unrest honour them, and is quixotic their persistence, in the same measure which their devices cannot finally elude the margin and the context of the analysis, in which sink all the attempts until being diluted. And it is not that there are not here very original and deep penetrations, although of different magnitude and draught, but which follows forbidden is the auto-definition, not being sufficient consequence of the analysis. But of what analysis?

§ 40 §

The waves that fluctuate with the proportion of *Phi (Φ)* can be added and simultaneously multiplied of non-destructive form, well-known property by those who generates radio frequencies for the amplitude modulation. In addition, *Phi* generates its series of powers automatically. This way, we see that the Continuous Proportion fills the real space of the waves in all the possible senses, whereas the waves of the analysis deduce real solutions of the complex plane. Thus, the Continuous Proportion is the true sea in which they sail, emerge and sink the real solutions of the analysis, the phase differences considered either as waves either as particles; but on the other hand the complex plane that defines the analysis contains these proportions like parts they are of the real numbers. We can ask how it is possible this.

Bergman created for the first time a system of numbers with irrational base, indeed the value of *Phi*, by virtue of its algebraic properties. A. Stakhov has generalized what it seemed a simple case and he has put on relief essential properties of the system. All the integer numbers can be generated with the set of *phi* and its powers, admitting a constructive and algorithmic treatment. This already is something extraordinary. In addition, new definitions of numbers for each one are generated of which a theory of numbers exists, being then possible a infinity of "theories of numbers"; the same classic or Euclidean system of definition becomes a "degenerated case" of the general theory. Therefore, we have an unsuspected new dimension in the density of the real numbers. The "all is number" of Pythagoras well would admit its reformulation in "all and everything is Golden Proportion".

The itself, the exact and generator number of Euclid, the Principle or Unit, is reformulated like *Phi* in this ampler and comprehensive meaning.

Between the new advantageous properties of the numbers of Stakhov, we have its possibility of ternary formulation without losing the favourable conditions of the binary notation, as well as a mirror property that allows to the test of the system itself thanks to the reflection of the generalized golden numbers and its powers in corresponding his counterpart of Fibonacci numbers: the Z-property. This reflection between discreet and continuous numbers or processes makes a entirely new *asymmetric theory of the measurement*, completely algorithmic, that can lead to us very far. As it can be seen, we are in front of an extraordinarily robust model whose implications now we began to glimpse.

This new order of the Mathematics also includes its own functions, matrix and a long et cetera. How it is then possible that its own density is not mixed with the one of the Analysis? If the complex plane is like the sea for the solutions and waves of the analysis, the measures of the Harmony Mathematics are like drops of oil that can possibly be united and they extend in the surface. The so called "harmonic analysis" of Fourier would have to be called without sarcasm "compound analysis"; the true harmonic analysis will depend on the modality.

The functions of the analysis trim their real values against the *sui generis* continuity of the complex plane, that properly never is outside; if, beyond the modality, and taking of the hand to Hegel and Gauss, we would define this in the old terms of dialectics, we would say that the being stands out against a background of non-being that at no moment would have to be alienated of its definition. That is indeed what happens. This "non-being" to be generated by the same functions it is outside them. Or more simply speaking, which is outside is the time, that is left into the hands of the logic. What the analysis cannot get up is the temporary asymmetry; however for the harmony mathematics this is something inevitable, since the Golden Section is the measurement of a in the habitual sense non-generalizable own asymmetry , but to which is possible to refer all the external or internal asymmetries like members. These are not only heterogeneous to each other, but that would have to be, by definition, heterogeneous with itself. Since *phi* can translate different patterns of measurement to each other, responding to the old problem already created by Eudoxus, the *Continuous Proportion* can be considered like the original module of integration. Like asymmetry already in act and with no need of a symmetry of reference, the Continuous Proportion admits the real time and what is irreversible in the mediation and the communication. But to take more far its potentiality we need a proper setting of real problems.

§ 41 §

Naturally, the Continuous Proportion and its closer ratios have been found in the pulse, the temporary intervals of systole and diastole, as well as in the maximums and optimal minimums of the sanguineous pressure. Also of very significant form in electroencephalogram, as well as in other miscellaneous rhythms of the body studied with different means and degrees of dedication. Its relation with the development, the three-lobular segmentation of the body and its gauges, and even with the asymmetry in the cellular division is well-known on the other hand; not to mention its roll still somewhat ignored in the modulation of the DNA. Aside from this powerful ubiquity, is impossible to value suitably the real importance of this module, since as soon as it is not said to us in relation to what it operates. It remains suspended in the air without hardly relating to another thing that to itself. However, which is absolutely evident is its aptitude for the optimization, its determining capacity of maximums and minimums *whenever they are referred to itself.* This can be a vicious tendency, but in fact it is already in this context that has become its self-reference evident. And in such sense, all the values related to *phi* must be considered like *self-values*, index of themselves. But this is not at all in discord with the spirit of the harmony mathematics. If on the other hand it has been wanted to appeal to the natural selection like sufficient reason of the surprising insistence in the appearance of these optimal values, is simply because it is not possible to go to another more ambiguous and general external reason. It always lacks a background. Even, instead of adaptation, it is possible to speak of the virtue of *adherence* of *phi* to the irregularities of the objects, of his fidelity to them. This is already the maximum criterion of selection, that other principles would try to imitate. However, From where it is made? Any theory that leans in the distinction between

[64]

the interior and the exterior is as primitive as to explain everything.

Either we have the great generalization of the Golden Section for the number theory, and it is time to advance a generalization to define its inclusion in the real time of the things and the entities. For want of experimental and formal development for this intention, we will be contented with the philosophical and qualitative definition of the subject.

§ 42 §

Let us think again about that great set of fluctuating biological rhythms that occur in our own body: the pulse, the electrical activity of the brain, the one of the skin, the breathing, the pulsations and divisions of the cells, the cyclical emission of determined bio-molecules, and a long et cetera. That all these biological oscillators have a concatenation and connection, is a fact as doubtless as the manifestation of life itself. However, the inter-mediation that is supposed between all these rhythms is so complex and detailed that hardly we would be able to understand it without loosing ourselves while we disentangled the maze. The question is if a scale exists that crosses all the scales longitudinally and in cross section, a generalized rate of the rates. Of course, that has seemed until now a chimera, in spite of the reasonable of the supposition. We have already seen that the Continuous Proportion gives an ideal mathematical frame us to make this correlation of measures, although by itself it is revealed insufficient. The Continuous Proportion is a module of integration of asymmetries like proper measures; it speaks to us of the measurement of any possible connection. We need a selection index to give us real connections. But, on the other hand, it turns out inadmissible to refer *Phi* to another thing that to itself, because it would supposedly cut the virtuous circle of its self-recursion. And speaking of circles, also we have seen that the connection of *Pi* and *Phi* is always fleeting and miscellaneous: what it already seems to say to us how mysterious

[65]

and subtle must be the nature of this self- reference. However, we spoke before of if there is something able to unite the rates of the different fluctuations, that something was the phenomenon of the form, the ungraspable and specious form. And of which the minimum signature for any specific modification of the form was the conjunction of the three modalities of the nature according to the Samkhya; what we applied to an oscillator like the pulse, the most primary and generic of which we can find in the body. Being the Continuous Proportion a purely formal reason, and giving us the Samkhya the more purely empirical and modal reason of the form like fluctuation, and being both inherently ternary, necessarily has to coincide in their own sphere, that for more abundance, is the generic circle of the oscillator.

§ 43 §

For the Samkhya the *gunas* are the last reason of the fluctuations and, therefore, its concurrence is necessary and of universal character. The only thing that changes from a phenomenon to another one are the proportion and the magnitudes, being in last instance the magnitudes also an effect of the proportion. What this would imply is that if we know the factors of the modifications in the pulse of the man, also we can know them in any other animal, and any other system that keeps analogous minimum conditions: the Sun is a great example for this class of analysis, even though to anybody escapes the abysmal difference of the conditions.

§ 44 §

All this would seem absurd if it did not find his natural hollow and its correspondence in dynamics. Matsuno and others have treated the commonly avoided fact that the third law of Newton referring to the action and reaction does not give us a reason nor mechanism for its fulfilment. The third principle would have to be the passage of the most general and abstract principles -the establishment of the rest and inertia, and the definition of force with respect to that-to the real world of the innumerable interactions. On the contrary, not giving it any material plausibility, it turns out to be the distinctive characteristic of his perfect isolation, simultaneously that guarantee and safeguard of the operation of the law of the gravity in the context of the game of the forces. What the third principle wants to establish and to consolidate is the dominion of an absolute time of global synchronization that necessarily evacuates the problematic of the signalling or the local communication between bodies or agents, really, the question of the information or mediation. That global synchronization, refractory to any arbitration or measurement, is completely conserved in the theories of special and general relativity by means of the transformation of Lorenz and the notion of covariance. The quantum mechanics is not either made question of it, fitting its cancellations so that they agree with the exigencies of the conservation principles. So that even if we want to describe in detail the action and reaction between two billiard balls that hit, the interface between two kinetic energies of input and output, the statistical or thermodynamic mechanics is included and explained by a quantum mechanics that ignores those problems to give back without touching it the balance of accounts to the classic mechanics. This way the principle of irreversibility of the thermodynamics, unique that can give account of the real interchanges of communication, is sent of return towards no part. Indeed the best definition of information, not to say the only one, is the one of inequality between an action and a reaction. **Local asynchrony is the only proper measurement of the communication or mediation.** Any other measurement is a remission to a composed analytical space; any interaction of waves or particles is a mediate attempt of detaching a principle that already has excluded the mediation. What we looked for, on the contrary, is the immediate and general form of the mediation possibility. And although we spoke in terms of the modality, is evident that the three principles of Newton are there for demarcating the field of necessary and the possible thing, without never entering the ground of contingency. A third principle never was more to the service of the other two, neither had less mediation capacity. Here is the strength and the independent expansion of the physics like discipline.

§ 45 §

If now we return to our fundamental oscillator, we can include in the game of the ascent and reduction of the waves the inertia and the force with the greater facility, and say in the same way that the principle of *action* and reaction of both comes defined by the perfect continuity from both, so that it does not admit nor it demands a specific location. For the ideal case of the ball rolling subject to a force in absence of friction, mass and force become indiscernible by definition.

The formulation that Newton makes for his third principle is extremely careful: "For all action there is always an opposite and equal reaction, or the mutual action of two bodies the one on the other always equal and is directed to opposite parts". The terms have been left free so that the term action can mean indifferently as much the transmitted force as the body with its mass; and when it is spoken directly of the bodies which among them it gives is not another thing again that its "mutual action". We do not know if the action- reaction really takes place between bodies or their actions and respective reactions. The action and the reaction include the mass and the force and can occur without another relation that the one of "action and reaction", indeed. In comparison, the most modern equivalence of mass and energy not even have been tried to explain, since it emerges already excused from the pure formulation.

[68]

We know that no natural unit of mass nor of energy does exist at the moment; and in truth it is completely improbable that such thing could be found out of the complex correlations, in view of the abstract character of such magnitudes. The force notion can *be made up* or compose sufficiently within the analytical framework, but also lacks natural units. We have already seen that the concept of "quantum of action" introduced by the quantum mechanics is valid only like measurement of energy-by cycle-second, being the unit of time arbitrary but irreducible the one of frequency. Of all this it seems to follow an important lack of harmony and correspondence between the different forms from expression of the magnitudes, arisen from the conveniences of measurement in the historical bifurcations of different problems.

In repeated occasions like fundamental unit of the mechanics has been proposed. Domingo Acosta, for example, gives us a definition of the mass like a set of impulses in all the directions and the speed like a balance between impulses in different directions: the impulse is always a unit of force applied during a time. Acosta is wondered if any force can occur or be applied independently of time, and reaches the conclusion that in the nature nothing similar can exist; we are of identical opinion. Grejzdelsky approaches of another form the same problem and points the convenience of replacing the ideal notion of absolute rest by the one of initial imbalance with a minimum value quantified by the constant *phi (Φ)*.

§ 47 §

Let us try to lead back these valuable indications to the subject of our oscillator. Of course, nothing forces to us to consider the impulse, as it is defined, like a natural unit; we simply considered it like a more suitable unit to our interest. We part of the principle that a simple harmonic oscillator is not indicative at all of a proper time, but of a reversible and completely unspecific time. Nevertheless, this one must serve to us as reference, or otherwise we would not know how nor by where beginning to measure the inequality in the balance or asymmetry in a given complex oscillator. But this does not mean that we leave from that ideal oscillator and we apply continuous deformations to it in the way of figure 9,

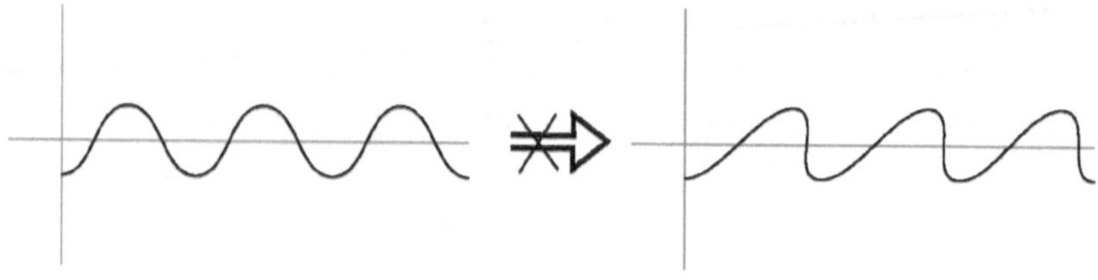

Fig. 9

then in fact, our assumptions go in opposite direction, although no definition of the impulse as force per time oblige us with respect to the cycles.

We can interpose with perfect arbitrariness a regular or linear oscillator in the middle of a non-linear oscillator.

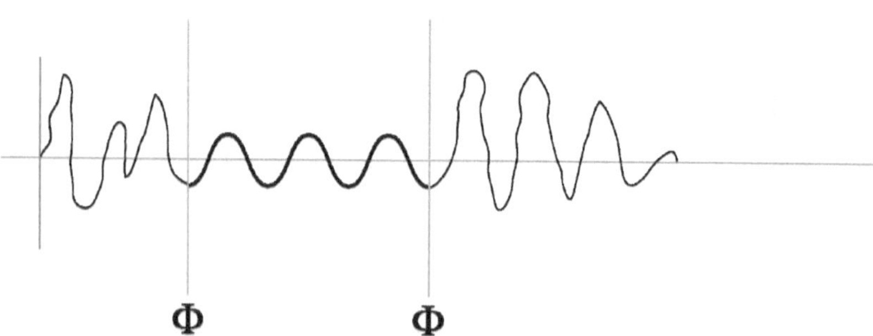

Fig. 10

We know that things thus do not only not occur in the nature, that cannot either take place such steep cuts nor in the best conditions of control. Aside from our manifest impossibility to imagine it, that denominated phase transition exists; that transition of phase includes as well diverse factors like the damping. Nevertheless, and beyond all it, subsists the fact demonstrated by diverse theorems that *Phi (Φ)* is the last ratio between frequencies and amplitude that its stability, although it only go by consideration to its "specific density" with respect to the whole and real numbers. So that the Continuous Proportion really is not in one or another part of the oscillator, nor in one or another of its phases, but along the phase itself and in anyone of its cuts, that which has come to be called edge of chaos. But in the same way in which the pulse allows us to accede to an inner section of the organism without carrying out the smaller invasion or cuts, the Continuous Section is inserted in the reasons of a process without it has sense to speak of inside or outside. It is already truly eloquent that we begin to notice so subtle thing.

§ 48 §

A balance between impulses can be conceived as well as an impulse with its proper time span, if we equipped to our imaginary balance with a time of adjustment between the successive operations of add and remove "weights"; time to which also we can grant variability. That is to say, we located ourselves completely in the asymmetric theory of the algorithmic measurement that Stakhov proposes as generalization of the classic case of Fibonacci. That estimation of the time interval between discreet operations gives us a measurement of the inertia of the same balance, or if it is preferred, of its sensitivity. The inclusion of this third element is necessary to obtain an exact correspondence. Since the moment in which the three share now an input of time, as much the mass as the force can be equaled with the impulse by means of the sensitivity of the balance.

[71]

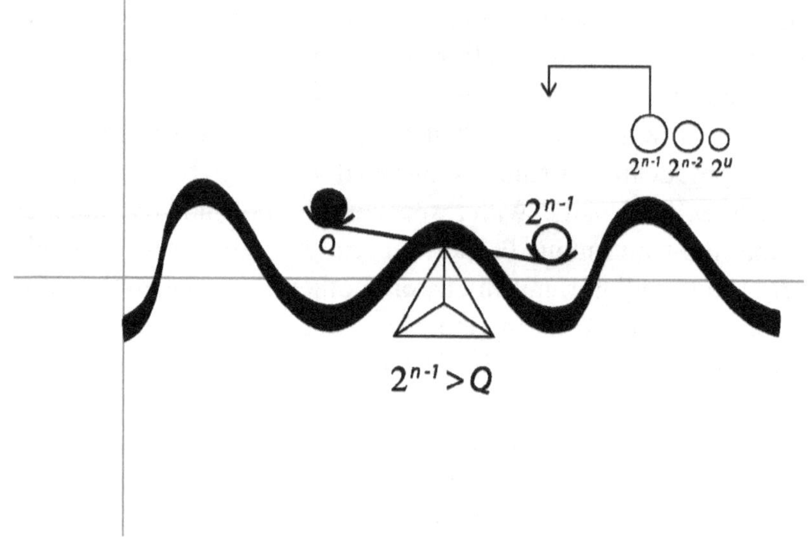

Fig.11

This disposition allows a more fluid and also operative conception of the problem of the motion in an oscillator, with no need to be refer to the sources of the impulse; in fact, which allows us is an absolutely general conception of the motion. The own time could then also be defined as the real and potential input of operations in an interval. The possible operations already come limited by the present loads in course and the weights available, that can be of different magnitude and proportion. This is, cannot conduct any operation in any amount of time. By incredible that seems, the physics does not take care in general of restrictions of this type, but of general much more relative to the conservative principles and constants, that does not touch the case. Without these restrictions, it is not possible to find a specific form in the processes. In addition, without these restrictions the conservation laws remain

[72]

unfounded as incomplete, and always more supposed than truly reasonable. Also it is doubtful to speak of the absolute energy of a system, notion that is surely indemonstrable by the absence of a fixed value of reference; but to deal with the energy available, only the real one, is used the absolute energy like reference. Therefore, a more conspicuous measurement of the energy must be possible. The notion of impulse and its adjustment in the temporary balance would have to approach us to it.

§ 49 §

The relation of Φ and Π in an oscillator is too ambiguous and open in absence of *proper weights*. In principle it seems too evident that the primary reason of a regular cycle is the maintenance of a stability, until the point of which cycle, regularity and stability practically sound to us like synonymous. The more relevant property of the Golden Mean seems to be the conservation or maintenance of the asymmetry or inequality at different levels, disappearing in the infinitesimal continuous to reappear by itself in ampler intervals, without another solution of continuity that the one that indicates itself like Continuous Proportion. Or in other words, the Continuous Proportion expresses the balance in the same imbalance, the self-sensibility as form of stability. This is the heart of which, seen from outside, it is consider like the problem of the optimization of maximums and minimums to us.

The Continuous Reason makes be worth the irregularity of the individual throughout the time, but at the same time the Circle would have to tend to annul the differences. Which produces friction on which? Both ratios do it and both can mutually be eliminated, eliminating themselves with it.

Little more we could know if they did not interact in a third ratio or property.

[73]

§ 50 §

Instead of loading our balance with impulses we can load it with the fuzzy weights attributable to the three *gunas*, or if we followed with the pulse motif, to the three *doshas*; the mass or inertia in terms of *Tamas*, the force of *Rajas*, the temporary sensitivity of the balance, an inertiality of superior order, like *Sattwa*. Naturally, the three appear already in a whole undivided set that as in the previous example tends itself to be not perfectly located and to assume layers of time span. The specific weights of the three *gunas* with their mutability would give us the values of *Epsilon* as the generic frame of not- linearity. Now studies exist on the presence of *Phi* in the fuzzy sets, and the relation between both is quite natural if we consider the mentioned "density" of the golden numbers and the problem of the over-determination or intersection of areas and spheres of inference. This would be the optimal experimental and formal frame for a definitive advance in the subject, and perhaps, to go beyond it.

§ 51 §

The temporary sensitivity of the balance can be graduated in diverse ways, and we will obtain different types of links of series or sequences; but more even than the type of sequence it concerns to us the possibility of expressing and of modelling suitably the phenomenon of the thickness of the signature in the characteristic *form* of the pulse. One assumes, and also this is essential, that this graduation of temporary sensitivity must also give us the relevant degrees of precision for each case. The "semiosis" problem, or infinite remission from terms to others, in mathematics the impossibility of solutions, is avoided because an immediate location does not exist, but rather an immediacy not absolutely located, that is an optimal adjustment or tends already to an optimal adjustment of terms, which sets out like intrinsic nature of the same motion.

This also supposes intrinsic or proper limitations within the interval. The infinite remission of terms throughout the optimal adjustment tends to be stumped or to cancel itself throughout the optimal adjustment; cancellation that never can be total and absolute, but more or less suitable or simply sufficient. From a technical point of view, this would be a new frame for the probability spaces.

It is evident that in systems under control the balance cannot "become crazy" at any moment, safe by the gradual or sudden destruction of that "control"; the biological organisms and the human being are part of this set of systems. Here the problem is not as much to find stable solutions, as appropriately to graduate the spaces from which the instability is pending.

Without doubt, we could not have found nothing more fragile and precarious to give account of the stability of things. We move in the tightrope of the pure conditionality. If this conditionality were not naturally softened in some kind of buffer, nothing would be possible.

§ 52 §

Almost without trying it, we have made a somersault. But we have still not landed nowhere, nor we know if this first twist is not only the first of an indefinite number. The used terms have corresponded of inevitable and natural form. Our tripartite definition of the impulse is, like the Continuous Proportion self-recursive. Also like in Samkhya: the inertiality can be computed like sensitivity, but not of immediate form.

It happens that if we can define the mass or inertia, the force and the action-reaction within the self-referent ratio for the impulse, also we would have to be able to make the same with other magnitudes or notions, like the tension, the pressure and so many others. Why? By the same reason we can make new definitions of numbers with its corresponding number theories, in infinite number, within the system generalized by Stakhov: that it is, in addition,

[75]

an algorithmic and constructive theory of measurement, with the amplest and precise criterion of analogical-digital convertibility. That is to say, we can redefine the magnitudes, the conditions or parameters, the constants and all the notions as we consider suitable. This is a luck of universal physical translator with its own rules of adjustment, their required logic and all the constructive means. With complete autonomy, and of such an amplitude as we do not find it in any other experimental discipline. If after this we talk about subjects like the compatibility with other metric and disciplines, it is simply because still we have not begun to go deep in which there is here. All the later references to other sciences and disciplines hardly are another thing than imaginary excursions to attract the attention on which it is not here revealed, in this new frame.

§ 53 §

Like the dialectics of the old times, the modalities of Samkhya do not express another thing that that of which nothing exists by itself. When we reduce this to antinomies or polarities, like the one of the cold and the heat, we cannot leave triviality; when we introduce a third element, which normally we cannot leave is of the arbitrariness, that allows to affirm and to deny everything indifferently. Even in the logic of Aristotle there are triangular contradictions of impossible solution, as Giorgio Colli underlined in his time. But these contradictions of qualitative order have always occurred by the incapacity to establish a bond between the qualities and the proportion, which on the other hand is something unavoidable and natural, and conditional also. If we managed to express that conditionality suitably, which we have is the key of that old and unattainable philosophical reason, the conversion of the quantitative thing in qualitative, and vice versa.

This cannot either get rid of the paradoxes, since the formalization, as the own form or the motion, never can be fixed,

[76]

but be managed or arbitrated at the most. But also it can transform itself with a defined rigor, and here we come into a new space of transformations.

§ 54 §

With these three components we have defined the moments, modes or fundamental modalities of all motion, although we left the ends of that definition *necessarily* loose here, what would require a special development. Nobody will be surprised of which here there are not analytical solutions, since which we try to go deep in what necessarily escapes to the analysis. The non-linear balance would be the more simplified analysis of the non-analytical in general. The principle of least action is present here fundamentally in the number of operations for a partial balance from moment to moment, not from instant to instant. This principle also may be in the number of weights of both "plates", as well as in the time of reaction of the balance that also can be comparable with the others. The motion, the resultant of these three ways, is seen necessarily surrounded by this third mode or sensitivity, to which in fact we can consider indifferently first. Therefore, which seems to surround to the motion is just the same that undresses it, and its lack of definition, its authentic proper definition, moving away of the ghost and purely abstract motion of the analysis.

A smaller time of adjustment of the balance, a finer and defined outline of the curve, necessarily does not mean a better or more optimal adjustment to the property of the motion, since also it can mean the opposite, a fragility, an excess of instability.

The question of the possible couplings between coordinated motions would seem to be indicated by the time interval that quantifies the sensitivity or reaction of the balance, being able to consider these intervals then as bars of balances on which to put other balances, forming indefinites series. It is always the mean part the one that evolves, the one that surrounds and fuse in its

[77]

limit the past and the future, the interior and the exterior, those predicates whose relation we excluded for the homogenous space of the analysis. These couplings or transitions of phase would have to occur even within the apparently simple systems, like the pulse or the undulations in the water of the sea, and have to be related to the generalized hyperbolic functions of Lucas and Fibonacci.

In all the modes of each proper motion we see that different possibilities of purity with respect to the form exist, understanding by purity the greater homogeneity within the greater definition or clearness. This notion of purity is more improper when it settles down by comparisons between different entities from the same sort, and more proper when it is considered from the scope of possible evolution of a single entity. Anyway, it is not possible to be denied that intrinsic degrees of purity, definition or perfection in any properly natural motif exist, either we think about the ribbing of a leaf, that has supported degrees in its development, in the spots of a leopard or whatever we consider. Intrinsic means that they can be appreciated in his own context, to which we simply we are giving a frame. We took to intention visual examples to make see that this same principle is applied to things and orders that little have to do with the visual appearance. We could consider it in the plane of the sound or any other.

§ 55 §

It is to be present that we are not taking care here of the general question of the compatibility of this model of the motion with the analytical space, thus we say, the one that we applied in a billiards table, which we left into the hands of the competent specialists. What demands our interests is to be able to define specifically the form of the motion in real time, leaving at the moment to a side the possible metrics of the space. It would have to be a fact that this form of the motion manifest in the most external appearance of a process or a living entity; and if this is true, the metric of which we considered outer space, a pure construction, would have to adopt other modules.

It is a serious error that still persists to consider the motion like something perfectly explained by the modern kinematics, also developed in the baroque age. Paradoxes as those of Zeno have been tried to explain by sum of infinite series of terms, something that surely nothing has to do neither with the motion nor with reality. Alexis Jardines remembers to us that exactly the intention of these paradoxes was justly to demonstrate the impossibility of represent the motion in the space, so that all these "demonstrations" and their acceptance continue being mainly ridiculous, simply a form of not wanting to see something. Jardines jointly subdue quantum kinematics with their limit of uncertainty and the relativist kinematics with its ambiguity or relativity of the simultaneity within the same classic case for the motion of Zeno, coming to say that both are the extreme illustrations of the same thing, motion itself, although do not try to give an operative model for this motion. We will say the same with respect to our model? We agreed with Gardens, and this is the fundamental thing, in that a single motion exists, independently of the scopes, or otherwise it would be vain to try any unification. But Jardines, with extreme consequence, radicalize a position that no science can assume, nor to digest: on the one hand, dynamics only describes the rest, and, on the other hand, a same object or process from different positions no longer is a single object, but different objects. In the middle of everything, the motion is intrinsically indeterminate, since the same time is a wave. The arbitration of a theoretical enigma already is a existential problem, and in this case, the solution is too threatening for any scientific notion of the reality. As far as which our model can locate in means between quantum uncertainty and the relativity of the simultaneity, or the ambiguity in the intervals, it can be said that in the first place we do not know the rank of validity for relativity, but mainly, which we do not know is the general compatibility of this temporary model with respect to the metrics of the analytical space. No of these things constitutes the immediate nor the fundamental thing of our problem.

§ 56 §

As we have characterized it, the motion has a surrounding aspect with respect to its moments, no matter how hard this surroundment is the own undressing of their form. In a identical way, also the mind adopts this surrounding character, and then **it is possible to ask if the mind is not another thing that the same motion**, motion that is inseparable of its form. Not only we create this, but we ask to anybody what another thing can be thought. It is not possible to think the mind but like motion, and if we resisted to it, already is by the own inherent motion of thought, reluctant to the identification or fixation; if in this respect we are forced to believe in other things, is by the absolute deficit that any representation supposes for the motion. It is more, we will say that to think that the mind is another thing that the motion, that already has all the necessary complexity, it is simple fraud. Soon the same space of the analysis pushes compulsively towards the vagueness and the inconsequence to us.

For Samkhya or Yoga this vagueness does not have sense. Try anyone to stop the mind and will see that one does not face another task that to stop the motion by the same motion, with its inertia, its impulse and its sensitivity. Here the things are recognized of first hand, with no need of any representation. But to all this respect, think about the spectacle offered by the western philosophy speaking of pan-psychism and the universe of *qualia*, and the *mind-body problem*, still following the Galilean scheme of the secondary and primary properties and completely ignoring that as much on the qualities as on the same motion the Indian philosophy had genuinely resolved the problem already thousands of years ago. This was only possible remaining naked in the problem and carefully avoiding all the trifles of the representation,

[80]

that after all, are only other forms and other clothes for the motion, and successively far away of the question.

Therefore, it would have to be the easiest thing in the world to find mental "correlates", since they exist in all whatever moves, thus is a piece of rock. Another different thing is to want to fill up the content of those correlates, which is not allowed to us nor even with our own mind. For example: if we want to carry out feedback with the waves of ours encephalogram in real time, rendering attention to the modulation of the waves flock any other possible content, no matter how hard these exist in the same motion with the form of inertia or other qualities. This is the basic deficiency of this type of instrumentation, simultaneously that simple illustration that the mind is the mere form of the motion. Therefore, it is not necessary to look for the mental correlates -and we do not say, sancta simplicitas, the consciousness- in determined groups of cells of the brain, no matter how hard also they are there: the only real location of those correlates exists in the time and the motion, its asynchrony or its synchrony, and this extends from those same nervous cells to the pulse, the breathing and the most external corporal motions. The same spatial, taxonomic location, has to depend in last instance of the pure temporality of the development, of which each act is a landmark.

If we consider the necessary couplings between the form of the motions that occur in our own body, we will have a much more resolving frame for the question of the interdependence of the body and the mind. Because if by one hand it is idle to think about the mind without conditions of motion, is not the same with respect to the materiality, that already in any case is conditional, and conditional by the motion, indeed. I don't want at all to enter in the subject of the independence of the mind of a given body, although in fact would have to be easy to see that this is not a real problem, being the problem the conditions of the form: for this it would be enough to see, far from any rhetoric, the binds and the unbinds that take place in the modes of the water of a simple undulation in the sea, as we are considering. As we said, the content of those correlates is something that is only incumbent on to that mind from its same condition, and in no case from outside, unless we have desire to waste the time.

§ 57 §

If the estimated weights of the three *gunas* become equal and they balance, momentarily and by definition there is no action nor reaction possible. This is, the *gunas* naturally conform an equilateral triangle integrated in the unit circle of a regular oscillator. But like the *gunas* can only exist really concatenated by the action and reaction of its difference or inequality, is clear that we are leaving outside the process of its proportional equalization, the optimal way that takes until there. We are leaving outside the Continuous Proportion. Relying us on our own categories, a circle and a triangle such could only exist outside the time or like an unstable moment without proper temporary duration, that is to say, they would not be able to manifest themselves.

§ 58 §

Nevertheless, we can see that the three *gunas* tolerate so much the character of cycle or circle as the self-recurrence with specific proper values. We have already said that *gunas* are anywhere as much inside as outside and that we can observe them if we learn to analyze what we see; that there is not another thing to know in last instance.

If the existence of *gunas* is based on its inequality, on the other hand it cannot modification or fluctuation without the dominion of one of *gunas* on the other two, which makes possible that that modification can be notice properly as a moment. That dominion has the form of a modification of the weight or value of one *guna* that reverts on the weight or value of the other two. This admits and demands characteristic sequences that, beyond the abstraction,

[82]

constitute the only form of causality which we can know. That is to say, there is no another one, and any other apparent form of causality will be revealed as devoid of form, like a correlation that must by necessity to be refer to the only form with its own modes; we can then call them degenerated cases of causality. All whatever that can become intuited is here.

One *guna* or modality cannot exist separately, so that a state dominated by *Sattwa*, we take as example, already includes the presence and subordination of the others, as much for the most stable cases like for the modifications triggered by the fluctuation. The same it is valid for the other *gunas*. We can say that there is no action without potential energy, neither sensation or sensitivity without action, but in no case we can reduce everything to the potential energy, nor to the action, nor to the sensation, since thus separated we would lose the reference or the mode. It must be clear that these ways are only applicable to the real cases, not to imaginary entities without comparison terms; it is by this that *gunas* are considered like genuine material causes of the mutations of the real, conditioned things. Patanjali distinguishes between diversified, undivided or monadic, only indicative, and non-indicative states of *gunas*. The same empirical or mutable ego is an undivided and indivisible state actually, no matter how hard so many insist uselessly on their theoretical dissolution; the pure sense of I, the existence like mere attention, is an only indicative state, *Linga-Matra*, reason why the non- indicative state or *Alinga* properly is un-manifested, rather than non-existent, if we want to fit expressions that not always we used with much property. This is, the state of balance of *gunas*, whether it is considered or not "metaphysical" term (which would have to include all the well-known reversible physics), not is attributable to it neither the existence nor the not-existence, and the only thing that is possible to say of it is that it does not generate indications nor references, nor terms like the previous ones that always have a fictitious element in their framework.

The fundamental states or sections of *gunas*, in their divisions in groups of six or five, have an extraordinary importance if we want to deepen in this dominion, although now we cannot get into it.

§ 59 §

If the balance of the three *gunas* constitutes its non-manifest state, it is because there is no place in them for the dissolution, growth nor decrease, since they have no further material cause. If we follow sufficiently the growth or manifest decrease of *gunas* in an entity or system it is inevitable to verify how values that seem to be diluted can emerge from their latency, and on the contrary also, which is in substantial harmony with the conversion of continuous and discreet values in the development of the Continuous Proportion. But a value cannot sink in the latency, relatively non-manifested, without passing through the modality of the Latency or Retention, that is to say, *Tamas*, in the same way that cannot emerge without action or *Rajas*, nor acquiring certain balance without *Sattwa*. Then, there is an eloquent continuity between the content of his values and the form in which they are manifested.

§ 60 §

Even accepting that *gunas* themselves neither increases nor diminishes, any action or predominance of one on the others in a empirical or temporary entity has to be seen in such terms for the understanding of the sequences. A sequence begins by necessity in the *guna* that then is already dominant. But this already produces a redundancy that can be detached indifferently of several ways, since what is increase in one always is a correlative diminution in another one. We can detach this of several indifferent ways, one of which would be:

1°. If *Sattwa* or sensitivity "increases", it entails a correlative diminution of the activity or *Rajas*, and never it increase.

(This does not seem nothing evident and there are many experiences that at first sight seems to contradict it). It can produce neither "increase" nor "diminution" of the principle of retentiveness or *Tamas*.

2°. If *Sattwa* diminishes, it can only happen by a correlative increase of *Rajas*, and never by its diminution. It is why the term *Rajas* is synonymous of contamination or dust. *Tamas*, as in the previous case, it is not affected directly by the modification of *Sattwa*, but already the increase of *Rajas* operates its diminution.

3°. The diminution of *Rajas* also corresponds to the increase of *Tamas* or inertia.

Thus they are included the four possible direct motions of *Rajas* or activity, and both of *Sattwa* and *Tamas*. *Rajas* is in the middle of the three *gunas*, and is the only possible connection between the other two. A defined order is conserved although what it seems beginning of a sequence can be seen from another modality like consequence, and the increase, like corresponding diminution, and vice versa. We move already in the circularity. Of course that we are not going here to advance the formalization and quantification of a system that seems insignificant and that in fact it is possible to be complicated of indefinite form, being able to deal it any logical with more pleasure and competence. Certain that it would be possible here to speak about disjunctive and conective functions, but we would prefer to adhere to which the nature is able to unite and to separate, which has a very different reach; we will return more ahead on the subject. Also elementary figures and diagrams with indefinite combinations can be obtained. Now it is enough with seeing that the order of *gunas* is simply a scale or ladder that simultaneously allows to the union by degrees and the separation or exclusion of certain immediate motions. That is to say, it is an elementary model of the mediation, that in itself admits almost infinite variations.

§ 61 §

Until now it never has been possible to elaborate a quantifyable model of the mediation operative in the empirical dominion, that can take us to some checkable knowledge. If we want to ask what makes it possible now, the answer is in all the previous one. Or if it is wanted to summarize, in *Pi, Phi* and *Epsilon*. It is necessary to say that we move here to look for, not the most exhaustive and powerful model, nor the most comprehensive and general, but the optimal one, that in the end could be most exhaustive and general.

We have then in this model an oscillator with purely quantitative elements, a scheme of the modalities that in their quantification even refer to the purely qualitative element, and a purely optimal element that even operating in contexts of maximums and minimums never can be considered neither quantitative nor qualitative. So that we have the elements for that balanced search of the problem of the balance in the plane of the discovery of the form.

§ 62 §

In this form, we can see how the three *gunas* correspond to a cycle or circle through their "continuous" mediations, whereas they demarcate "discreet" sections defined by the exclusion of determined immediate reactions: the interaction of both throughout the time for the real cases will demand the inclusion of an optimization term whose more generic reason will be always the Continuous Proportion.

§ 63 §

The observation and the self-observation with respect to our context within *gunas* always would have to tolerate more lucidity than mere illustration with "examples", which would not have to be there to add themselves simply to the general case.

In any case, in relation to the sequence of *gunas* we can think that we can become from a state of lucid attention to another one of estupefaction, forgetfulness or inadvertence without continuity solution; but it is this type of sudden conversions the one that makes impossible the same nature of *gunas*. Without a doubt it must have had emergency of other thoughts or impressions before whereas mutations, although that modification whereas thought has been able to arise from the loss of the balance and whereas impression could have been a loss of inertia in form of released latency. This could as well trigger a series of reactions amplified until a new modality becomes dominant, in this case a certain unconsciousness. In the same way, the increase of activity cannot be in itself the cause of the pleasure, but by the momentary liberation of a determined weight of conscience or unconsciousness, giving passage to diverse sequences. The fundamental nature of *gunas* dominates on what is accidental of the reactions, but that is not so easy to see without considering the specific weights of the situations, that, in last instance, refer to a native constitution generated by alien forces and an apparent cut.

In fact, from the possible sequences of *gunas* and all its impossible mirages we could derive all fables of the myth and the cascade of the literary forms and its contents.

§ 64 §

Always there is to be possible the distinction between the momentary balance and the constituent, that goes progressively being altered by the first, of entirely analogous way to as *vadya* can clearly distinguish between *prakriti* and *vikriti*. Without this previous landmark we lack the valid reference for later inferences. But both factors already are undivided in the form subject of gauge, in this case the pulse, reason why they are considered by its mutual reference; what implies as well an active balance whose value is given by the same motion within its own intervals.

[87]

$ \S\ 65\ \S $

By opposite that can be to the perspective contemplated by the thermodynamics, as well as to a discreet mechanics that cannot solve entirely its foundations, the temporary irreversibility in non-ideal processes exists because the complete loss of the information of the previous states does not occur; that is to say, because it is not possible to be eliminated or to be suppressed. If it is considered in diffusion terms, any loss or liberation to the "outside" of the system will correspond with the consequent reactions in the interior, and to this it is not necessary to give many rounds about it: rounds that we give it in fact taking advantage of the virtues all type of cycles to eliminate the signs. From the quantum of action (whose cycle is omitted), to the most virtuous biological cycles erasers of the information -the only one that there is, the one of the previous states. The impulse notion that before we exposed demanded a temporary interval, interval that can be spread and be emerged based on different potentials. But it seems already lamentable that we must resort to mixed terms with those of the analysis to make reasonable what by itself it would have to be evident. We arrived at the situation in which the most demanding reductionism is incapable to do nothing with a mechanism as obvious as the circle, because it is incapable to apply it itself. The determinism tends to be applied so on nature in a way that we remain undetermined, and what at first it could be a Jew-Christian prejudice has gotten to be with time the decided search of a situation of maximum advantage. The India philosophy, on the contrary, part already of that situation in which to find advantage is an impossibility, and in addition is undesirable.

$ \S\ 66\ \S $

Perhaps the principle of minimum action is most general and including in nature. It has been said that this principle cannot acquire relief precisely by the differential context of the analysis, but this cannot be but part of the truth. The analysis seems to benefit enormously from this unexplained simplicity of the nature, simultaneously that seems to adapt it; what it cannot happen without something very fundamental has been relegated. The optical ways of the light, in the refraction of a ray in the water, for example, are understood like minimum routes because they run by the way that spends less time. Nevertheless, it is more than doubtful that a natural phenomenon can be directed by a temporary principle of economy, only imputable to certain subjects of the men; at the most, this could be an indirect effect and collateral of another disposition of the motion in time. In other words, if we considered the existence of "atoms" or waves of time, these would not have where to go: so it is the concept of modification within a sequence for the Samkhya. Concept that besides is not incompatible with the quantum mechanics, although this one cannot contemplate it because it does not leave site him. **The "action" defined by an impulse tends to last in the time in the maximum extension of the sequence or sequences.** Yes, this seems to us an intrinsic property in the nature in addition to harmonic with the perspective which we are contemplating. By the way which it is not necessary to make a great exercise of etymology or *nirukta* to notice the relation between the word *krama*, sequence, and *karma* or action: *Karma* or action is not but the round circular figure within the sequence, also in harmony with the nature of the operations before alluded.

§ 67 §

Thus, the principle of minimum action or the minimum, or optimal ways, acquires a relief very different from which allows the differential calculus to it. But it happens that what is contemplated in the analysis of waves is the change of phase and not the same phase. Contrary to which often one assumes, the uncertainty principle does not prevent that we could to register changes throughout the phase; the limitation only exists for the spectroscope and the Fourier analysis. Numerous types of sensitive detectors to the phase exist, some of which are even used in colour televisions; the only limitation for its sensitivity is the capacity to eliminate the noise. Naturally, this does not contradict the uncertainty principle, but it allows us to obtain another type of information that can be more relevant in other contexts, like that we propose. On the other hand, the quantum theory does not contemplate things such as a component of acceleration for photons, nor modifications that can be equivalent in another context. For regular oscillator of this type, that do not admit real fluctuations, neither the non-linearity nor the other meaning of the principle of least action have nothing to say.

§ 68 §

If, as limit case, we could completely make external one to each other the five elements of the pulse, we would have a pentagonal symmetry like which so very insistently we have in living beings. We could to use fuzzy graphs, but these elements and its values always will overlap, never will appear exempt, as they do it in the more patent way in the external form, that for the rest, if we followed it in its order of generation, takes us to the Continuous Proportion. The pentagonal symmetry has been in all the cultures incarnated symbol of the microcosm, of which it acquires differentiated laws amplifying a very small or infinitesimal difference, but never unsubstantial. The hexagonal symmetry, however, has been always symbol of the balance of the macrocosm: not of its closing, but of the ideal interpenetration of the space and the time in its three respective dimensions. We cannot then oppose both symmetries as they oppose the organic and the inorganic; because for physics, that deals with the conformation of the forces in the inorganic in general, these three dimensions of time do not exist properly like slopes or tends, but like unspecific and arbitrary distinctions. By the same reason the dimensions of the space are made a whole undivided that becomes mere support of the infinite

[90]

directions of the vectors, without on the other hand it finds specific principles of direction.

The hexagonal symmetry is then epitome of a principle of least action more inaccessible to us than we think, and the diverse levels of the pentagonal symmetry exhibit the laws of persistence of the differences. Both seem fundamental to be able to understand the relations between the singularity of an object and its insertion in a vaster scene. The theory of regular solids will hide for always so many contents as those that we are able to formalize, and that why a mathematician as Felix Klein considered the regular icosahedron like the mathematical object with more possible connections.

§ 69 §

It seems also evident that the most intimate aspects of the sound, related to the harmonics, the material implication of the timbre and the resonances, as well as music and its sequences, can be deal with more explicit and different form, without for a moment leaving the scope of this extended classic mechanics. The same stairs of the modality, the conditionality, are a musical scale, even if eludes our representation and our ear.

For the usual classic mechanics, the sound is a mechanical wave that needs means with a density for its transmission; for the India conception, the space and the possibility of being crossed by the sound are the same, soon are not needed means transmission and the problem of the emptiness or the ether is indifferent in such sense. What defines the problem is the aptitude of the receiver, its sensitivity. The receivers adapted to the resonances in a planetary system would be the own planets, and if we do not know to model the conditions that make them sensible are because there is no space for it in the mechanics to the use. Perhaps the appropriate rank of precision or definition for the mechanics of this system is inseparable of the radii or diameters of the same planets, whose average orbits would represent whole numbers, although to consider

[91]

this without another method of analysis is completely arbitrary. As for the rest, something as well as "pure dynamic resonances" cannot exist, which is equivalent to a pure fiction; if there exist resonances they have to have an acoustic and net mechanical character. The Pythagorean music of the spheres would not be a metaphor.

§ 70 §

If this model of motion and fluctuation fructifies, we would have to be able to apply it of an appropriate form to all the things that move and fluctuate. Departing from that, we could posse necessarily the form in which the different motions can make contact, friction or coupling. This is, can be considered in vertical different changes or phase transitions, no matter how hard these are not simply affection by the verticality or hierarchy, and since they have a certain diffuse aptitude to reflect a complete and self-sufficient set. Supposed the universality of the form in the motion, this is applied without rank distinction, whenever they are satisfied minimum conditions of description. So that the connection between the different subsystems from a given system could not only be study, as it is the case of the biological oscillator, but that also we would have the way to appropriately compare the most dissimilar and separated things by its characteristic forms of motion through the general constancy of the form.

§ 71 §

It does not seem that could be made use of this proverbial Gold Cane to measure the things with inadvertence of which those measures mean and involve, which provokes the doubt that as well really their use is given to us. Here we would enter for the first time a dominion that surpasses our notion of the analysis as exhaustive study of the alien, separated things like objects. We are not customary to it and most probable it is than we try at all costs to formalize it like something without direct implications. But also it is certain that it has been an increasing process of formalization which has taken to us up to here.

Let us try to imagine what the application of these categories would suppose for the economy, for which has been called "economic analysis". Everybody admits, beginning with the same economists, the technical impropriety of the tools, not to mention its incompetence; in spite of which they are continued applying with the great power of those who pretend an absolute technical superiority. The reality says to us that that superiority is based exclusively in capitalizing what it is made suppose that is the only measurable and the observable, that is to say, in the imposition on great scale of the same categories whereupon the analysis takes place. In spite of everything, it is necessary to recognize that it is the whole genealogy of the analysis, and not only the economic one, what has lead to that state of things in which already are certain privileged criteria.

What is what will fit those who tried to fit everything? The extended motif of the balance already is the most generic form of transaction, simultaneously than its more acute indicator; from now on also we can use it like symbolic interpreter, without it lets depend on us the purity or fits of the interpretations. A strict and consequent analysis of the economic curves would keep awake, in the first place, that the denaturation of the economy begins by the intervention and distortion of the cycle of the cycles, the currency. From here all the consequences for the theories of the balance can be followed in cascade for the general distribution and balance theories, until now little more than dependent macroeconomic notes of those control "constants" of the employment, the interest and the money. The consequences of the application of the model of partial balances would be often so strange, that it would be necessary a good time to purify the concepts and to undertake actions. By the same reason, the application of the model to the coupling of the different sorts of activity would be essential.

It is not necessary to look for examples or enumerations of the fields to which it could affect this general vision, because what we are treating is the overflowing of the classical methods of the analysis and his fulfilment in the particular.

As we said, it would be comfortable to maintain all this in the tolerable margin of the theories of the complexity, but the fact is that affects the same hearth of the analysis, without meaning of objects. We can then ask which is the relation of our idea of the analysis with the physics, that great symbol of our commerce with the reality. The answer, that already we have advanced, is very simple: if the physics takes care of forces that do not fluctuate, in that same measure our concept of analysis does not have anything to say. The Samkhya is the specific analysis of the fluctuations, whatever they were. Therefore, which we have to ask is which is the relation of the physics with the fluctuations. This relation is expressed in the variables and it is limited by the constants, that can be of very diverse ranks. But the changes that express those variables are in principle and by definition continuous, even though they come from discreet changes, reason why also the relation with the fluctuations is weak and unspecific, and accidental in any case. Yet, it is the constant notion that seems definitively to limit the dominion of the fluctuations. The most fundamental constants talk about the forces, the speed and to the definition of the least action; the non-linearity is of side although in fact it can be in the middle of the others of multiple non-explicit ways, deciding its relation.

We have already seen the character more limitative than complete of the definition of the quantum of action. As far as the speed of the light, often its variability in the context of the space-time sets out, contemplating, for example, also the possible variation of the fine structure constant of electromagnetic coupling. With respect to the gravity, the first great constant in order of appearance, any mention of its variability is always seen with incredulity, and its interaction or fluctuation with other forces is so weak that hardly could conceive something about it.

§ 73 §

But in fact it is easy to see that the physics has needed the constants for its constitution. If the gravity, for example, had a variable intensity, the calculations and extrapolations would not be made difficult, but practically impossible, at least within contexts like the present one. In addition, this could affect the rest of the constants. Often remarkable variations, much greater than the factor of relativist correction, have been detected in systematic experiments with graves objects in the same Earth and even in a same place; not to mention the estimation of the masses of some planets of our small Solar System. But, in absence of a correlation factor that has been considered acceptable, such variations are refer to the little precision in the estimation of the mass of the Earth -what it is surprising enough-or to any miscellaneous factor that are possible to suppose more than to find. It would be absurd to hope that the physicists could renounce to their precious accumulated capital if there is no clear possibility to still win more; not in another way the scientific knowledge is managed, and nobody is to be blamed for that reason. There is no doubt that such fluctuations would stop being ghost if could be worked firmly with them; but this does not talk about the *what* or the of the implied factor, to physical causes, as to the whole form to practice the analysis, to its procedures or methods. What, for many, it is still worse.

§ 74 §

Someday in the future it will seem to us incredible that our ancestors clung to as improbable beliefs as the universal constancy of the gravity and other forces; and until we can be asked by virtue of what means it could not seem improbable already to the same Newton.

Before answering this, it is necessary to recognize that the present attitude of the physics already invites to pose the problem. The hollows generated by the idea of the constancy begin to occupy too much space, although, perhaps in a comical way, is wanted to fill with new material causes of the most improbable materiality: thus we have the dark matter, the dark energy of the "cosmological constant", or another version of that constant in form of multi-compound scalar field to cause the masses of particles. These three problems, leaving of side other many existing ones, are referred to the scalar component additional of the vector magnitudes or forces, leaving at the moment unaffected to these last ones; what has the appearance on a desperate attempt to preserve the invariance more suspended every day. The scalar fields arose in the middle of the XIX century for problems, so alien to the classic physics, of the thermodynamics and the mechanics of fluids, and is also improbable that they can be applied to a greater resolution without forcing by counterpart to a dissolution of the rank of constancy or action. That is to say, the scalar fields, also usually denoted by the letter Φ, the only thing that can obtain is a *local adjustment* of the functions, which already puts in interdict its constancy in the space and the time. If this is applied in addition to the mass as to the gravity as much, the problem of the stability of the solutions as well as the absence of really applicable minimum units of measurement are elements that mutually tend to scuttle. This is equivalent to say as much that we are in a transition of phase for the same form to make physics, as for its contents. And the test is that nobody has the smaller idea of how fitting the components of these fields. The pretended constancy of the forces and the masses to which they are applied is more and more at the mercy of the fluctuations of fields that, like in the hydrodynamics, hardly could be modelled. The situation remembers vividly to the one of a small paper-ship in the sea.

In addition to all this, and in intimate relation, are questions like the one of the hierarchy of forces and constants that makes possible the "fine adjustment" of values as dissimilar as the gravity, the masses of particles and others so that they make a universe so relatively stable as this in we live ours. But this cosmological perplexity, whether related or not with that "anthropic principle", it is not but an indicator of the extreme conditioning which that initial exposition is subject; aside from which already it is more than doubtful that we could to calculate the improbability of this universe lacking the suitable units for it.

In the same way, one have more than reasonable right to doubt that matter has identical characteristics and fundamental values wide and long of the whole observable universe. This is the same class of assumption that with the constants. Of course, something we know on the limitless capacity of variety in the nature as to believe without remorse in a monotony introduced only for our convenience. Certain that there is monotony in nature, but how different from the uniformed normalization of the analysis.

Diverse variations have been proposed, like for example, the one of the length of the radius of Bohr of atoms, using this one like reference and cause of the relativist deformations, in addition as local clock. But if we deepened more in these and other alternatives, we would always arrive at the consideration of which only the local variations can give reference frames to us, instead of considering the global uniformity (cosmological principle) like guarantor of the constancy and equivalences. Briefly: we cannot decree the universality, that from that moment would be empty, just as the rest of the so called "democratic principles". **There is no another universality that the one that can guarantee a stability of the local conditions.** Thus it has been always, it is, and it will be. In the meantime, it is necessary to remember that does not exist any theory that guarantees the stability of the matter and the atoms beyond the exclusion principle, that the same physicists tend to consider like secondary and somewhat phenomenological, although that depend on the context in which we could to frame it. This context is not clear either for physics.

In such conditions, one does not know why we allow ourselves to speak with as much familiarity of the matter, that, by definition, would have par excellence to be the locally conditional and most contingent thing. This is, would have to be able to be treated like the most faithful indicator of our contingency with respect to any other possible states, whose partial occupation is surely one of the best reasons of the existence of which we called universe.

But, leaving to a side other things, the same atomic theory has sectioned whole parts of the behaviour of the matter that can be observed and measured, and that often and incidentally remerge in the context of the "exotic states of the matter", virtually infinite. One of the greater limitations of the atomic theory is that it only contemplates extremely short times of reaction, escaping in this way many transitions that are equally relegated to the phenomenological and miscellaneous. The stability of the matter can only be determined comparatively by the form of the reaction curves before similar stimuli, and the criterion is the same one that unites and separates *gunas*: in what extent diminution of the own action is defined by the retentiveness or sensitivity gained, and to what extent the increase of an own action generates or is generated by one of the other modalities. In order to define such own actions the logical thing is to begin by sensitivity to the stimuli.

§ 76 §

The discovery of the inequality in the cosmos, its variety, will cause a impact much more deep than which caused in its day the expansion of the spatial and temporary perspective. Watched well, such expansion had more of theoretical movement of generalization that of real inclusion, and therefore, affected more to the imaginary than to the possible action. The change that is being experienced now is the one of the local insertion of the phenomena, just at the moment at which everything seemed forced to uniform itself by the requirements of the global definition.

§ 77 §

At no moment its universal generalization of the gravity could seem to Newton a boldness: in the context of the analysis, the gravitation became general by itself and by necessity. The organic reintegration of the law of inertia within the superior framework of the three laws or principles of the mechanics, without doubt the greater profit of the absolutist physics of the baroque and the physics in general, was enough. One would say that that great speculative moment, so clear in the philosophy of the age, has been perpetuated of unsuspected way in the physics until beginnings of century XXI without getting to become totally aware of itself. In the three laws or principles the notion of absolute time or global synchronization is already implicit, but only outside them it has his place to become explicit; just in a parallel way and without contacts as like the Samkhya defines the situation of the modalities or *gunas* with respect to the absolute awareness or witness,

Purusha. But if after all Newton arrived at the total trust in the exactitude without limit of rank of the law of the gravity, as well as the absolute time, being both as unjustified proposals as Metaphysical, it exclusively had to the intrinsic nature of the analysis or infinitesimal calculation, and to no other thing. The absolutist prestige of the universal gravitation must *to the space of the analysis*, the only form that can give expression to it. This means that beyond this space the universal gravitation does not exist. Some conscience of it could have Newton himself obstinating so absurdly with the subject of the authory of the differential calculus.

The historical fact is that Leibniz was the first in making public a mature concept of the calculation, and was not mere

[99]

chance. While Newton could handle it before, it is well clear that what was worried to him was the own defined solution of his problem, created in net geometric terms. The ease to generalize the calculus, that the same form of the annotation exposes, demanded sufficient independence with respect to the materiality of the problems, which was not given to Newton. Leibniz perceived in addition in the potentiality of the calculus a whole orb of problems and a perspective that no but he himself could suspect, and that still today wait to be correctly raised. Therefore, the autonomy of the space of the analysis is born with him and no other, indeed because Newton became their maximum applicator, and only in a slope or direction of the problems that this space raised.

The space of the analysis "has invented" the universal gravitation, not vice versa, and this explains the irritation and the mutual misunderstanding in this extraordinary knot or controversy. No distortion will erase neither the truth nor the weight of this fact.

§ 78 §

Already it has been spoken too much, although never with sufficient sharpness, of the perfect antithesis that composes these two counter-figures of the baroque. For example, with respect to the election of the principles, that in Leibniz shell in a plurality that tends to be annulled by its competition, and that in Newton are organized with such an economy that even today our incompetence to penetrate them is revealed. Leibniz wanted to found his whole philosophy on the modality, whereas the principles of Newton exist exactly to evacuate it. The mechanics of Newton has a fully plastic appearance and is so convincing for that reason, although as we have seen, this is exactly appearance. The dynamics of Leibniz or its monadology continues being interpreted indeed being so badly seen like plastic, that is to say, under the glance of Newton, when it is evidently a musical order par excellence, a thought order to cross the appearances. Most of the philosophical subjects of Leibniz continues being interpreted of very pedestrian way by the aforesaid reasons, and is for that reason that the most advisable form to approach them would be indirectly, through the empty space left by the same Newton.

§ 79 §

The pre-established harmony of Leibniz, for example, that seems most of us the *summum* of the gratuity, if not of the arbitrary, acquires relevance in the same and exact measure in which we realize of which the absolute time of Newton, the global synchronization, is not less metaphysical at all. And not only that: if we perceived the net metaphysician character of this last one, we began to understand or to at least suspect that to which Leibniz is alluding with the question of that pre-established harmony is exactly to the possibility of synchronizing entities and processes that already are asynchronous, since it is of themselves who derive their own law. But on the other hand the monads not even exist in the space, but that are location principles, as much with respect to the space as with respect to other many substances or planes. In the same way that only for asynchronous processes can have something to synchronize, exists the non-located for the locality, of a form that in the space only partially can have tracks. It was the same Leibniz who defined the same point like pure modality.

§ 80 §

The monad in Leibniz is already the best figure of which he understood ideally by integration; more than the defined integral, the indefinite sum of terms. Also this distinction lacks any value for the modern context of application of the analysis, but not for the context of the monad , neither in its affection, nor in its modality. In fact, the monad is the space of integration par excellence of all that that now we called non-integrable, no matter how hard the question of the not-linearity could not be considered then. For that reason Leibniz introduces the principle of least action and the optimal ways, in a context and with a reach that little has to do with which in optics could notice Fermat. The characteristic calculus did not aim either towards the rudiments of a logic of propositions, but rather towards the revealing of the non-divisibility through the ways in the individuals. We could extend with other reasons like the one for the discernibility, the necessary fuzzyness of the perception, the fracture of the real sequences in our understanding, the idea of the representative like sufficient index and not like representation space, the mere incompetence of the mathematics to choose between different descriptions of phenomena, the correlative motion and many others; it is difficult not to see the full unit that surrounds to these motifs, that, if remained in fragmentary notes, it was as much by the technical incompetence of the time as by the absence of minimum required sensitivity. The moment of all this was very far, and the mechanics already gave problems enough to work.

§ 81 §

The idea of the constant is a superstition generated by the effectiveness of the infinitesimal calculus, and the later developments have only contributed to prop up it. Of course, also it has been an enormous utility, in addition to indispensable work hypothesis. The restricted frame of the analysis has prevented any serious effort to resist this idea or to handle itself with its variability; on the contrary there have been made all kind of efforts to isolate these values of "disturbing influences", rejecting with it an essential part of which it constitutes them. There are then good reasons to consider these constants of so many decimal numbers of precision as mere statistics that fluctuate with respect to something unrecognised or unknown.

[102]

When these values so fantastically precise occur us, we can only ask how many things have had to be left of side; without a doubt this bonds for all these displays of precision in the analysis.

§ 82 §

If physics is an indicator of our commerce with the reality with secondary repercussions in our imagination, the theory of the evolution is as an indicator of our commerce with the imaginary, and even the fantastic , with not at all despicable consequences on the reality. Both are needed as the left hand and the right, but not being able the physics to conceive another thing that limits, and being the evolutionary theory incapable to conceive the limits of anything, the joint impotence of both to define any thing that really concerns to us is manifest.

If something has been misunderstood and even ridiculed within the philosophy of Leibniz, that has been the call principle of the best, than often it is reduced to that on which we lived in the best of the possible worlds. Since we have had neither balance nor weights to resist that affirmation, we cannot either know not even to what is talking about. As it already noticed Ortega to this intention, the famous affirmation does not mean in fact but that our world is the less bad of the possible ones. What concerns then such proposition are the intrinsic limitations of the things, of the set and of each one of them: its own imperfections. The only possible teleology, the only legitimate study of final causes, only can talk about *an empirical disteleology*, that is to say, to the study of the imperfection in the nature, of its inherent limitation, non extrinsic. They are inconceivable the one without the other, and both must find their sufficient expression (that not their sufficient reason) in the form of the motion.

We excuse to say that this has been completely unapproachable for the evolutionary theory; and although this one tries to defend itself of the teleologism and of the context of the final causes,

[103]

the certain thing is that without this it becomes a pure episode, anecdotal and irrelevant. To whom they really interest last million or thousands of million years if they do not have no relation with which from now on it can happen? It would already for that reason only lose the relation with the present. The theory of the evolution cannot be allowed to be transparent to itself.

§ 83 §

And the same is possible to say of physics, that today is constituted through cosmology with evolutionary arguments, when its ideality and sustantivity are based exclusively in which it can be defined of a non-temporal way. Between both great branches does not exist the smaller real contact, but, simply, what it is necessary to suppose to us.

The physics can not absorb in itself neither the reference nor the meaning. We have seen yet that the three principles of Newton exist to exclude absolutely the modality, to evacuate it, although that is virtually impossible since the necessity is a modality. The plane of ideality of the principles of the mechanics corresponds, in the scope of the sections of *gunas*, with the exclusively indicator plane (*Linga-Matra*), that is privative of the pure sense of I or *Mahat*, to differentiate it from the mutable and empirical ego. This plane is the one that, directed towards the more differentiated sections, behaves like generator of the fiction, whereas its fictitious character only is reduce before and in the direction of the own un-manifested balance of *gunas* or modalities, the only state that it does not indicate nothing nor needs it. The balance only can be reference for the imbalance like its own internal space. Repeating it once again, Newton mechanics has already excluded the balance from its internal scope, and thus they have continued it making all the later developments. On the other hand, it is to note that the metempiric ego to that we alluded here continues being simply a state more of nature, and thus we must see it inasmuch the consciousness

[104]

without qualities is omitted. This implies as well most intangible but inevitable of the questions: that a state or modification is defined upwards or downwards, towards its qualification or disqualification, can depend as much on the conscience as immediate instance and for that reason unavailable-as of the same mediation of the qualities in its own circularity. Naturally, without some class of immediate knowledge the knowledge of the mediation is impossible. This it is the inescapable context of any possible evolution, including this one of science.

§ 84 §

Let us repeat once again that without a mediate principle of action and reaction our world slides magically in an absolute vacuum or nothing.

The third principle of the mechanics eliminated the friction definitively. Do we realize what this means? The thermodynamics tries to be explained by a reversible quantum mechanics that again fits its balance appealing to the classic mechanics, another reversible system. The mutual incompatibility of the sequence jumps at sight. The friction magically is erased again, being transferred of an unreal scope to another one, in an endless process that cannot never be filled. The one of Newton also was a somersault, that conceived like a landing, with the known consequences that still today good heads being are wrecking their necks. Considering it a landing, little conscience could have of the nature of the jump, that was imposed to him for the preservation of an acquisition, the discovery of a law. We have already seen that this one is insignificant in relation to the rank of the principles, so that it was a bad investment justified by the availability of mathematical assets. What now it has been exhausted is that availability by the expenses that it itself has created, so that it is not left more remedy than to return to the principles disinvesting as much as necessary. The problems with the scalar magnitudes are thermodynamic problems, of imbalance or irreversibility only because this is what it has been evacuated; in other conditions and with other principles the same irreversibility would adopt a completely different aspect, because it would not be dissonant. The tri-modal analysis is also applied to these three great moments of the physics, where unfortunately the physicists are obstinate in seeing only two. But here it is idle to do juggling between branches to match that already have become different by pure exclusion and convenience: the only worth is to give with a undifferentiated object of the suitable rank and to adhere firmly to its possibilities.

§ 85 §

The same it is worth for an evolutionary theory, that as Peirce saw, can be reduced to the three moments of chance, statistical selection and habit or conservation. This last one was translated in XX century like genetic inheritance, a reduction that the time is showing like too insufficient: the gene concept has been evaporated and there are no simple forms to explain how the genetic inheritance is modulated. More than programs, the genes begin to seem what really they are, considerably integrated construction materials.

In the same way that in physics, but in an incomparably greater degree taking advantage of the inherent complexity of life and Biology, there are an infinity of appeals to one or another contiguous instance -chance, selection, inheritance-without respecting the minimum logical order of the sequences, so difficult to arbitrate here, as for the rest. But it is the same, because in fact any mechanist explanation of the specification of the biological forms, when the smaller principle for the same forms does not exist, only can be a nonsense and an absurd, lacking of any sense of the property and the elegance. And indeed, the theory of the natural selection is only an appropriation of which it is not understood by the most inappropriate means. Besides, it is necessary to say that not even the most complete theory of the motion and the form will have never too much to say on the origin of the species, an imaginary space that is not incumbent on to us and that never can be fulfilled. The evolution in real time of the systems and living forms is thousand times more instructive and beneficial for us.

§ 86 §

The Samkhya little must say on the consciousness, since it is the reason for its development as much as it goal; in any case it seems the summit of ingenuity to limit the awareness to a mere subjective condition, when these already is for us pure possibilities whose limits nothing we know. By the same it is desirable to avoid to its respect all objective association. Then it is not necessary to look for where is the consciousness with respect to us, which already it is impertinence, but to see by it where we are. With the little effect that is wanted, this is what it has been said from always.

§ 87 §

As much the impotence of science as their value is show to us through the reaction that provokes the *hollow Earth* fable, that perverse and of course grotesque new edition of the cavern platonic fable. If somebody says to a scientific, instructed spirit, that the Earth in which we live is the convex surface of a bubble within an infinite rock ocean, we can believe to us with reasons to laugh at the extravagance; but if, as we argued descriptions, observations and data, we verified that our interlocutor is able to pleasing invert all those arguments in detail, the scientific, instructed spirit undergoes invariably through the foreseeable sequence of sarcasm, irritation, indignation and exasperation. A fatal moment arrives at which it must argue the details in the motion of the poles, and if the contradictor spirit also is able to invert this argument, it seems that it is not left another instance of appeal that to bore the Earth to sufficient depth, which at the moment is far from being

[107]

possible; although not even we know here, would say our ill-fated contradictor, if, in case that formidable sounding did not find where to stop, new theories would be invented on a space-temporary expansion of the rock.

We don't need to take this very seriously seeing that the mathematical laws and descriptions are always susceptible of arbitrary inversion; that the experimental data are it much less, but than, if in last instance they come defined by those mathematical descriptions, also will get to be inverted of one or another form. The hollow and convex Earth only reflects the autism of science, its incapacity to talk about suitably of another thing that itself, and that is denied to it to recognize by its lack of own reflexivity, of a space for it. Fortunately almost nobody, nor the same scientists, have hoped that science served the man to as reference. And nevertheless, what drags and what rhetorical.

Until now, science has lacked a self-reflexive space, no matter how hard it forces reflection as much to us if we located ourselves contemplating it from the outside as if we were applied in it: both moments become irrelevant for this because they are mutually self-excluded, which on the other hand will recognize any scientist given to make a little of philosophy in his free moments. If the knowledge of science cannot be valued by the same knowledge and has to be sent to the applications and to the horizons for the action, we always have science without conscience that uselessly appeals to the external ethical considerations. There is more conscience or unconsciousness than the one of the same form of the procedures, and is too vain to appeal to the conscience of the society for the scope of the applications or the mere consume if there has been no conscience when with the greater care they have been instructed and plot the protocols of the investigation.

Day to day presents to us more urgently the question of what we can do with our knowledge and the why of our dependency of it. More than to be able, this class of knowledge begins to seem to us shipwreck and misery. For that knowledge, the miserable dependency and the lack of self-esteem come to be confused in the same, and thus they let it know to the knower when it exerts like so and not as poor instrument.

The same scientific knowledge develops an addictive circle: once we assumed anyone of its marks, we felt compelled to make all type of questions, when on the other hand we never would have made the questions that already arrive to us like consequences. We must respond to questions that never we had raised, and this drags to us. We, who so superior we can feel before a farmhand that did not know that the Earth is round or turns around the Sun, had never discovered this by we ourselves, nor so at least us we would have asked it. In itself, our knowledge is of a fragility so, that it would have to induce us more to the fear than to the trust, not to mention the security. Any mediocre man can dominate and harvest the lights of all the passed enlightenments, but at the cost of the freedom to make his own questions. The history of science is the madness to accept a bet that cannot be won; at the moment this madness has not been instructive to us.

In addition, the exuberant growth of patterns that we believe to see in nature has resulted in the proportional impoverishment of our sensitivity to perceive them, until the point that to speak of any direct perception it has to sound to us unavoidably like a fable, or to clumsy translation of some underlying mechanism or highly refined pattern. Our imagined balance it would have to teach to us why this does not have to be so, and that we can well have forgotten to balance the weights. Refinement and dullness can go perfectly of the hand.

§ 89 §

In these circumstances, one can consider seriously if, more than an increase of knowledge, on the other hand inevitable, we rather did not need a way that guarantees its correct elimination. In opposite sense, the compression of information, that exists in addition to limited it is self-defeating. But Compression of the knowledge? Perhaps one did not say whenever "knowledge don't need place"?

That knowledge is based in the possibility of forgetting the object of knowledge, in an independence with respect to it. The elimination is the guarantee of the assimilation. The knowledge cannot be compressed, can be condensed, thicken, only leave sediment, by virtue of the process of independence of the object, and this not only like consequence, but from the same beginning. It would be possible also to ask for the retroactive effects.

An inverse relation between formal knowledge and the knowledge of the own form of an object can exist, so that one increases by the diminution of the other, and vice versa. The problem of our balance is located already in the middle and in the edge of that question. What would be to wish is that the problem as a whole simultaneously admits to be expressed with the maximum formal pertinence that leaves in the middle a continuous hollow in the middle and with degrees for its de-formalization, for the pertinence of the proper form, for the most intuitive and direct perception of the object and of we ourselves. Only in such case we could accede to an optimal and own form for the condensation of the knowledge, condensation that as for the rest occurs continuously in fact even hardly with some conscience or direction.

That the synthesis of the formal knowledge is often possible is demonstrated along the centuries; but whenever that has become reality, increasing the abstraction, has not made but increase as well to the possibility of dissipation or dispersion. They do not seem to be then very stable syntheses. If the possibility did not exist of leading back this towards the immediate or intuitive knowledge yet we would be lost; but until now that form of renewal has amounted in interfaces and technological products, with the proliferation of media and their masking, hindering the intrinsic and inexcusable of our own mediator character.

§ 90 §

The balance with series of adjustable and self-adjustable weights and temporary sensitivity are already the expression and the possible simplest symbol of this internal convertibility of mathematical structures and sensitivity. This model cannot be surpassed without entering completely in the absolute absence of form, of which little can be said; so that it is given to us like mediator. This can be known with no need to enter in the scopes of solutions of the problem. The simplest and intuitive form of any real problem, in economy, psychology or physics would have to be expressed and including in it. It is possible to ask if all the real solutions of functions constructed in the complex plane would not be degenerated cases of this type of real function, whose proper density also we have seen that it differs from the one of the analysis.

But this is secondary things. If this model does not serve so much to educate the sensibility as to make calculations, it would be necessary to judge it of doubtful or null utility.

§ 91 §

Here we are only presuming the existence of solutions for this type of functions basing not only on its majority, but also on the immediacy that the given real case with respect to the possible solutions represents. These must admit different sets of weights based on the definition of the time interval. As in the minimum non-analytic interval there are equivalent sets, *the diffusion* or expansion of the interval will define as well a function for the adjustment; and

[111]

thus we see as the non-linearity entails its own non-locality. This is not only one limitation, also is the proper setting as much of the problem as of the solutions, whatever it is the form that they admit. The touchstone continues being if there is some combination of the general problem of the balance able to describe the complete *form* of the wave of the pulse.

In the context of impulses that we have given, one would say that any process is partially non-located, and that the tendency to be located or to find its own or proper location is what conforms its existence. The location of the fluctuations is always a temporary phenomenon, no matter how manifold are the external factors that affect the system.

§ 92 §

This model of the balance, formally based on the asymmetric principle of measurement discovered by A. Stakhov, and materially concerned by the weights of the modalities, would have to be able of being expressed with such simplicity that a child of ten or twelve years did not have the smaller difficulty to understand the rudiments and perceive the implied principle or principles. And although coming from the world of the formalised objects that it can now seem easier to simulate in a computer, has to be inevitable to catch the very intrinsic of the motion, so that it is possible to be perceived more naturally and outside of control spaces, of which always is to leave. In the direction of that exit it would have to be always education.

§ 93 §

As well as the last nature of *gunas* only can be elucidated assuming the perspective of Samkhya, only from the mathematics we can get to conceive the possibility that the nature and the world

[112]

necessarily is not written in mathematical language, releasing us from that perspective in which we have confined ourselves from Galileo. In fact we know that it can be indefinite descriptions adapted to a section of the phenomena that can be mutually non- consistence without that affects for anything the march of such phenomena. We have already seen that a fuzzy system of inference can entirely describe a complex process with no need of differential equations. In this respect it is necessary to say that the applied theories of measurement in these cases can be different also and generate contradictions between them. The principle of asymmetric measurement seems to release of the arbitration or election problems of to us.

Perhaps it is possible to advance in the understanding of the independence of the reality with respect to the mathematics turning the formal necessities into necessities of material implication, and although this already implies formal operations, the important thing is the possibility of convergence in front of the constant bifurcation of branches of mathematics. It is more than doubtful that the mathematics ever had a central problem, but rather a fluctuation between reasons. Perhaps it cannot be of another form. The central problem that cannot be posed is its relation with the existence; the relation with the physical and measurable reality is only the end that leads without a predefined continuity to that other greater question. We don't need to say that for the India philosophy the being is independent of any formal superposition. That independence is the centre of convergence for the mathematics, the point from which radiates its necessity or non-necessity. However, this that seems a ultimate perspective has all its material implication in the problem of the balance, of which surely it is possible to demonstrate that it has decisive connections with all the important branches of the mathematics, and, in the most general plane, with the moments or interactions of the arithmetic, geometry and algebra. Therefore, it is possible to propose this problem with all its implications like the subject of the convergence of the mathematics. The questions of consistency raised by the logic or axiomatic remains like exterior and more purely formal to this one, if it is that the inconsistency is only the external aspect of the impropriety. As for the rest, when the logic assumes proper temporal modes enters conditions of material implication. This would also open a breach in the rampant abstraction of the algebraic forms.

In general, and fortunately for the rank of the mathematical task, the convergence of the mathematical forms depends much less on formalization problems that of the problem of the appropriation of the forms that we call understanding.

§ 94 §

Also it would be to hope that the problem of the balance throw light on the question, now entirely fundamental, of a more complete definition of the always slippery concept of potential, with the implications that this has for the physics and the topology. What it is not known is to what extent a sufficient definition would be compatible with the now habitual concepts.

§ 95 §

The computation has become "the natural" scenario to fight with the complexity, but at the cost of increasing the complexity and the autonomous sensitivity of the other scenario, it is not known if virtual or real, but in any case in motion. Without a doubt there are many areas of computer science already sufficiently developed that have not reached a greater integration by lack of development of the suitable object of reference, everything which is intimately united to the privileges granted by a conception of the analysis as narrow as little restrictive. The notion of modelling top-down and from the effects to the causes, as well as the programming directed to objects, tends to invest this tendency, but with too ample and still general approaches, caused more by the convenience of the procedures that by the direct light which they receive. That is to say, they are still blind tunnels, of which often nor one hopes that they see the light. This would have to radically change with the new class of object and process that we are redefining like the objects and processes par excellence of the analysis. Around this definition it orbits a variable constellation of elements that by themselves have never reached a critical mass, but whose set not only must exceed it, but also to generate another very different light. Between these elements we can include of more or less miscellaneous form the fuzzy logic, the algorithmic asymmetric theory of the measurement, the ternary principles of computation, the new kinds of analogical-digital converters, the variable architecture and re-programmable circuits, the relation between computation in parallel and asynchronous circuits without clock-cycle unit, the languages between objects, and the progressive thickening of levels in almost any interface. As much inside as outside are reasons enough to put in motion this orgy of complexity, but without a reference that can be simultaneously physical and formal they can only proliferate outside situation. The funnel of convection for all this storm, the so call "artificial intelligence", cannot be but another proliferation without limit of formalisms looking for to find its own frame. To call it "mechanical intelligence" would be an humorous term; nevertheless, without a mechanics that contemplates the degrees of sensitivity in its interior and knows to take advantage of them congruously, we are ourselves led to the proliferation of intelligent agents in the less intelligent of the perspectives.

But in no way agrees to make a joke of our increasing dependency and symbiosis in this unforeseeable and fuzzy scenario. The dense networks of the information and the tendencies in their configuration acquire of increasing way the function of destiny, Nemesis or necessity for that other social function that it is suppose that have to model them. On the other hand, artificial intelligence, that more than a defined object is the process that would have to fill and to crown this interaction, is purely synonymous of autonomy, the only concept that confers an own right and weight on it. So that we seem to be looking for the autonomy of the whole process of interaction absorbing all reference. To this almost indescribable situation it tends to respond our exposition, knowing full well that by the same form will come given the effects. The attempts to avoid the physical supports derived from this persistent tendency are deceptive and destructive; self-destructive, also.

§ 96 §

Known it is that two superposed glass sheets throw a number of possible trajectories in the reflection that adjusts progressively to the succession of Fibonacci. The most powerful means of calculation whereupon can be dreamed, the quantum computation, are only disguised analogical computation that looks for a digital yield, in the same way that the Feynman path integral is only the principle of diffusion of the light of Huygens -of all the points to all the points by all the points-with a finite speed for the light. Therefore, and ignoring incompleteness of the quantum mechanics and the analytical un- definition of the motion, the quantum devices will depend on a crucial way for their usable yield as well as for the discovery on relevant algorithms on the questions on conversion analogical-digitalis raised by Stakhov with regard to the Golden Section, in addition to the physical ones raised by us with regard to the motion. It is not either necessary to extend on the absurd of the interpretation of the quantum mechanics like the updating of all possible worlds, another form to evacuate the uncompossible to imaginary worlds. In fact all interesting and genuine of the quantum computation falls of the opposite side, in the evaluation of uncompossibles, of the mutual incompatibility in general. It becomes evident the inertia of the present analytical notion of the calculus. This makes also think to what sophistication levels it is necessary to arrive sometimes to return to deal with the most sensible, immediate things.

To what extent the confusion with respect to science, and to contemporary science in particular arrives, it is illustrated by the topic so frequently repeated that it comes to say that the Newtonian science was "hierarchic and theological", whereas the present one "destroys hierarchies and finds order in the chaos". The opposite is almost the certain thing, although, not to simplify in excess, it is possible to detach: "Newtonian" science is the less hierarchic than it exists, and in that exactly its absolutism is based. We have already seen for what the three principles of the mechanics exist. The modern science to which topical refers, the heterogeneous disciplines of the emergency, the evolution and the complexity, which does indeed is to create hierarchies, levels and meta-levels where more likely there are none, and everything because they are incapable to accede at a level apparently simple constituent level like the Newtonian one; as far as of the order of the chaos, still we are hoping to see it, if it is worth the trouble to speak of it.

But what is certain is that as much one posing as the others run like chickens without head. It is necessary to leave the soft fantasy of which both methods are complemented, since they would do the classicism with the romanticism. No, because a single meeting point does not exist, but lines that are superposed to different levels. Let us see, For what we want so much "fangs and claws" if the third law of Newton not even allows the friction? A mechanist *explanation* of the life, they say. What we are playing? It is simply impossible to maintain the least intellectual respect by this arrangement of things, excused product of the collusion in the specialization. We began to verify the power of the disjunction.

Without a doubt the evolutionism and all the phases of romantic science have benefited enormously from the credulity generated by the amplest emptiness of the analysis, simultaneously that the faith of this one increased in view of the food that the contents or the temporary matter promised to incorporate, without having the least foundation for it. Its already time to resist these hopes, to see what they weigh in the balance. A delicate operation.

§ 98 §

But, it did not leave by chance all modern cosmology in the most involuntary and unexpected form, by the instability that Friedmann discovered in the relativist equations of field? The same Einstein hurried to tie the ends with his famous cosmological constant, but by some mysterious reason, it was decided to find an experimental evidence of dimensions not less cosmological in the equally famous formula of the Hubble expansion constant . Constants or reasons both not less specious than the same *Phi*, with the great difference to fit in a well defined metric space. Pity that we do not know if the suitable one.

From our perspective, that small imbalance shot a unjustified compulsion to fill it; although from the perspective of the physics of then and now, defined fundamentally by the vector component of its space, it had not nothing more justified or necessary. The vector space of the forces is a compulsive space, without the smaller metaphor, since it is a space for the necessity. What it is never known here is the cut is made to obtain that section or slice of necessity, because the space of the analysis is in this respect a real whole. From here the convenience of using the notion of impulses in a temporary interval, no matter how hard they have all luck of doubts on how fitting them. Without a doubt the force notion seems to have the advantage of an immediate meaning and a net defined construction; we can print with our hand a determined force to a ball or another object, but determine the internal time that it requires the arm to produce that force, that already seems to us circumstantial, and even external factor to the force that we want to define. But if which we treat in cosmology is of the own internal time to the cosmos, if we cannot really escape to the Plotinian conception of the cosmos like a great animal because already we

[118]

are within, the things decidedly change, and our concepts of force, by well defined which they seem to be, can be perfectly like a slap in the emptiness. This space and this time are completely extrinsic and hardly they are immediate for no longer. In addition, not even they are constructed on a space of real numbers, but in reference to an imaginary time in "a complex" space. It does not seem then that such extrapolations deserve the credit that has been granted to them, and of course, which they do not give is the least security. In all this annoys the enormous difficulties to define clearly the potential energy of the gravity by the necessary conversions in kinetic energy; thus, the convenience has been expressed of considering negative the gravitational energy in terms of general balance. But what is certain is that the gravity, according to the circumstance, as much creates as destroys energy, and there is no extrinsic form to stop this problem.

As far as the logic, known it is the little value that can have for the physicists lost between so many timeless equivalences. If general relativity subtended a potential field to the unfolding of the vectors by means of an imaginary time, is possible to think that the introduction of an own, proper time in its real space would probably absorb and eliminate so much the construction of the space-time as much as the not less constructed force-vector notion.

§ 99 §

The space of the forces is a space of compulsion and necessity. But an indefinite number of scopes exists in which the necessity don't compel nor limit the evolution of all type of processes, that nevertheless perhaps makes possible. It would be necessary to excavate in this well of the possibility to see what time really marks the pendulum, the one of the necessity; and although this seems a rhetorical figure, the case is that we have means to do it. In any case, the imaginary world of forces that we have illuminated is an obtuse and brutal world because it lacks

[119]

in itself the necessary selective or restrictive principles. This is a world in which there is no a specific time neither for the actions nor for the things, which cannot be the more physical and materially false, and aspect of which the only thing of which we can be sure is that we ignored nearly everything. The times and the frequencies of the denominated quantum world cannot be sufficient reference either nor mark by themselves the hour of this clock. Beyond the limits supposed and compounds, if the space of the cosmos seems to us so fatally empty is by the enormous hollow that the physics has in the centre. The forces depend on the time, not the time of the forces; this is something factual, besides to be implicit in the laws of Newton. The equally factual inversion that this demands, corresponds to the new concept of analysis that we are aiming.

We don't need to say that if we put some emphasis in this is as much by the highly destructive character that the uniformation of time as by the compression and increasing location that operates like reaction. That temporary compression, so manifest in the scope of the computation, but tensile to the set of the mediations, is the same one that begins to reveal to us *per absurdum* the temporary friction and interferences between the successive actions and interactions, its diseconomies and uncompossibility. This it is already the inescapable context, only a veil of the necessity.

§ 100 §

Another error of perspective or world view to which often we felt forced by the disparity of the two classes of science is the one to consider the increase of the complexity like indispensable condition of the development, the evolution and even the consciousness. In general it is easy to see that the complexity tends to the restriction of the degrees of freedom of a system, not its increase. On the other hand, are genomes much greater than the one of the man in as simple plants as the irises. No of these two facts of so different rank serves to conclude nothing, but they at least force to think to us in relation to what there is to consider the complexity and the development. We don't need to think much to recognize that it is enough grotesque to consider like reference of the complexity the number of elements and its degrees of freedom, which already assumes that it includes everything, although in fact not even rubs the problem. Think in the degrees of freedom of atoms of a fly and those of the Sun. The restriction of the degrees of freedom is in this sense much more significant. Here there is already a great condensation as much of the necessity as of the contingency — thinking from the context that assumes these sciences—, so that there is no admissible reason that could explain how that double narrowing results in that widening of the possibilities for the living and varying watch of the fly.

In principle it is necessary to recognize that the complexity little has to do with the perfection; on the other hand, the notion of perfection is not contemplated –it does not sense- in the theories of the complexity. But if we admit that the complexity is immediately contingency, and of the mediate necessity we do not know practically anything, well we could admit that the intelligence contained in a brain could be more elegant lodged in a stone or a portion of air. In fact this class of arguments has little of joke, and of course they have material pertinence, because we do not know how much of our brain is absolutely necessary or unnecessary so that our own intelligence exists, far from it we have no criteria to find out it.

Aesthetically speaking, the perfection is considered the opposite to complexity and friend of simplicity ; and the genius, that twisted perfection, is the capacity to extract simplicity of the most complex and spoiled circumstances. In effect, it is the updating of the contingency which redeems the complexity from the scatology.

We here send to the subject before mentioned of the disteleology, the only context in which the perfection idea can acquire content, and to the questions of non-analytical balance or analysis of the balance. The ratio of ratios, the Golden Section, already is contained in the purest and more immediate conceivable form, so that aesthetics in its more fundamental and primary sense cannot be excluded. It happens that, of that pure form, we only extract mediate sections necessarily referred to the first that we are looking for although already is given. Inevitably it comes at the top the perturbation theory and calculus, no matter how hard the used references are not commensurable in principle.

§ 101 §

The universe or the manifest world as much has to be more intelligible when from the smaller number of causes follow the greater number of effects; that is at least the essence of the scientific program from the baroque to nowadays. From the position of the analysis of Samkhya, nevertheless, all the distinctions between measured and immediate things finish being diluted in the arbitrariness with total consequence: because for Samkhya the most located and immediate it is already the object of the analysis. Like in the famous image of the Indian string, it is enough to follow the end to lose oneself in the sky; *rope* or *string* is as for the rest one of the first meanings of the term *guna*.

So that the small artifice which we have mounted and unfolded with our balance only finds their reason of being in our approach to the immediate thing, and only by its immediacy other subjects are related to it. We have passed over the relation between the Continuous Proportion and the modalities or *gunas*, but although nobody never demonstrates its univocal relation will in any case be always and inopportune and the improper thing to disassociate them. The question is not as much the explicit nature of the relation as the mutual implication at the time of conceiving the modifications and giving frame them. One is pleased extraordinarily that this relation remains in general as non fundable or non demonstrable, because otherwise would not arise but a new space for the compulsion and

[122]

the coercion. If something had of divine the divine proportion, would be exactly this.

§ 102 §

To explain and to define the mediations of the world or the world like mediation is more than impossible, an interminable and vain task, in the sense that it makes us waste the time for more urgent things, in addition to in the sense that the later extensions will demand the destruction of previous marks. If this has not taken place absolutely, is because the extensions have not had sufficient span.

When Hegel undertook the enterprise of a general philosophy of the mediation, he only could justify it putting into play to history, the spirit, and all luck of upheavals; and he had good reasons for it, because everything indicates that even it is not a proper task for the man.

Science from Newton seemed to have drawn for before all that problem by means of the laws of the mechanics, whose immediacy we have considered, and in special for the third principle that had to define the mediation. And if Newton had had to give explanations on these three principles, it was not had less lost in all luck of justifications, not being, indeed, because such laws already justified a fact that emerged now with rank of superior law. From it there was that law of the universal gravitation the one that became creditor of justifications and explanations, when rather it had to pay them, but not to those who assumed its frame already, but to the principles that maintained it.

Being the frame of these principles immediate, but putting itself to the service of the mediation, there is no possible end or aim for the sequence, because if we considered these principles like a triangle, will still admit in his interior almost an infinity of congruent or incongruous triangles according to the case. We return to repeat it: to give account of the mediations of the world

[123]

does not seem a proper task of man, except for which the man has of mediation yet.

§ 103 §

For that reason it is so insurmountable and surprising for us this starting point of Samkhya to lead back all the mediations to the immediate without previous warning nor necessity of justification, with the most accurate and concise of the criteria. And surely is this position which has prevented to ours of being able to consider Samkhya like a genuine philosophy, when in fact it is the first and most solid of the systems that the philosophy has given, and surely already was explained with total consequence in the times of learning of the young Pythagoras.

§ 104 §

That Samkhya has an exact, scientific and mathematical background, in addition to universal, is something that nobody that knows it will dare to deny; another thing is that we have not guessed right in conceiving its frame more satisfactorily in two thousand five hundred years. This exact and genuinely mathematical character, the Samkhya can allow perfectly to ignore it because also it leaves it back, deriving from it an unquestionable superiority. Nor that to say has that the frame we offer here is the most external possible, in order to permit to the experience the way to fill it up. As far as the use or abuse of the formal manipulations for which field is opened, only the same development can decide where the legitimate thing begins or finishes. The treatment will have to find in itself the adjustment term, with nothing to guarantee the balance.

§ 105 §

On the other hand, the Samkhya as soon it has nothing of technician or scholastic. Its irreducible and primary vision would often remember to us to the ingenuous philosophy of common sense, if not were because the consequences cannot be more far from it. In addition, the conscience of the ambiguous character of the signs cannot arrive at a more acute degree. In a Patanjali aphorism he affirms that the separation of the sound, the meaning and the ideas produce the understanding of the sounds of all the beings; what here one assumes is the confusion and habitual superposition, as well as the feat that marks its real separation. It is easy to see in this a general reason for the same operation of *gunas* and the possibility of its motion. This is exactly just like the old hermetic axiom relative to the three principles: "You separate and purify it, that nature will look after unite". In this the analysis consists. In such circumstances, the knowledge is filled up by the same nature. This has an infallible reach.

§ 106 §

The ternary principle of separation of powers has known great fortune in the West, and to make sure it is not necessary more to see the joint of national and international, political and economic organisms. Here they have connected fatally the illustration and the esoteric, because it is not indeed for letting to do to the nature that organizations were created. It is the "ousting principle" of Newton for the modes what works here, which makes suppose that also here the continuous reforms with the introduction of new modes could be possible someday.

$$\S\ 107\ \S$$

Speaking of ousting principles, without a doubt everything what we are considering has remarkable relation with the static physics of the antiquity. To locate a modification is like locating the archimedian point in a scalar field that it does not admit fixed supports. The scalar fields, the last and definitive frontier of physics, simultaneously support and reference for forces of which never it was known when they were sectioned of the reality, are referred as well at the real time, at *the dense moment*, that which was evacuated of the thermodynamics. They only can be limited of explicit form, non-inherent, in the same way that in the self-recurring transformations of our notion of impulse for the balance, which always demand an arbitration.

$$\S\ 108\ \S$$

Affecting the harmony mathematics of the way in which it does to the theory of the numbers, and to the theory of the measurement, and to the relation between constants, variables and references – conditions- in physical processes, there is no of our great patterns that cannot be modified until the unrecognizable or the suitable. The least we can say is that from the situation of present closing already that capacity is had lost. This affects our concept of clock, to the units of time in the different processes, to the measurement of the information or power units, to the cycles and economic units including the currency, to the organizations and the interfaces between different processes and agents; so it includes practically everything. We can see the Continuous Proportion as the strategy subject par excellence.

§ 109 §

But all this is the instrumental context that would be so desirable to reduce. Samkhya and the Continuous Proportion show the thread to us of something as improbable as an univocal notion of the analogy, understanding by analogy proportion, through the certainty and constancy of the form. In this, that the pedantry of the modern intellectuals has considered impossible, resides nothing less than the possibility of an immediate and universal knowledge, and even simply the possibility of knowledge. Any problem of translation is inseparable of material conditions, that already are formal because they are conformed to a modularity. And when one thinks about a universal interface, also it is to this door that is calling.

§ 110 §

Any inclusion or coupling of this or any philosophy in the course of the necessity can have nothing of necessarily good; good only we can do it, and it is never known why or for whom, which matters so little for the case as it concerns the tree for whom are their fruits. On the other hand, to reinforce something with the speech of necessity only contributes to make it more contingent, whereas to catch it in all its contingency elevates the rank of its necessity. This is so certain for consciousness, that it even supports our vain games of words.

§ 111 §

Any science incurs the rhetoric when talking about to the Nature when it is clear that it only talks about itself. In fact, this appeal to the nature exactly finds its sense when alluding what it continues being left outside our knowledge more or less submissible to arbitration and arbitrary arrangement. In addition, so that the nature serves as substrate or support to the laws that we could to attribute to it, unavoidably has to also presume itself its complete indifference before these same laws, or what it is the same, its execution in the most perfect ignorance. The same form of the objective knowledge is what forces this type of consideration, independently of which is problematic or not. That is to say, within the objectivate, separated knowledge, there is no place for the consciousness in the execution of the laws because we have put all the conscience; but what it still remains independent of those laws it cannot become aware because if thus outside would not be susceptible to be satisfied to new laws that we could find like of forced fulfilment. What this means it is that any idea on the nature within this context is forced to the presumption, and is incapable to conceive nothing, and therefore it is of absolutely hollow and rhetorical character. Or more indeed, not even there is hollow or space where we could fit nature, safe, like in chance, by our pure ignorance; after all, a positive means in which we act.

But if someday we wanted to consider beyond the laws and the rhetoric to what it responds the expression *Nature*, we would see that there is no another answer possible that "to unite and to separate", at all on the conceivable levels and scales. There is another business nor no permanent activity in which it can be involved; and if these two or three words sound to us too generic, anyone will be able to verify that all other specification that we look for will already make in damage of the generality and property what we could to understand with the word *Nature*, and therefore, will not find more legitimate neither less hollow verbs that these "to unite and to separate". Less hollow, because the reach of that union and that separation will always go beyond the order that we are considering, being to this to which the well- known saying talks about of which "nature never remains idle". These terms will be always true beyond the reach of our knowledge or ignorance; one can be sure of it, as it will be never of the true "nature" of a force or a law identified by our own intellect. Therefore, we repeat emphatically that another definition or less rhetorical concept for the Nature that this one of "to unite and separate" does not exist, and only by this we can use this word with some justice and without using it like figurehead of the divinity.

Well, this "to unite and to separate", these three things, it is exactly what express the Continuous Proportion or Golden Section in the simplest mathematical way, reason why this explanation of which we understand by Nature –the *Prakriti* of the Samkhya-still is more opportune and still less rhetoric. Because we can be asked what is what to the theoretical physics or the theory of the evolution like scopes of "union and separation" contemplates, and to see to what extent they are in this respect circumstantial and sightless.

In the physics, for example, it is very easy to see the gravity and the radiation like epitomes of the union and separation, but what we are saying it is indeed that such union and separation are all-embracing, at least with respect to so net sections of the reality. That is to say, the phenomena of separation in diverse scales with respect to the gravity, and those of union with respect to the radiation are presumed. But this already is implicit of multiple ways in the same physics, so we are not saying anything new. Or maybe yes? The same mechanism of absorption and emission generalizable to all particles in the fields would already seem the least expression of this union and separation: but nothing further from it, in fact. Because the physics is already constructed by means of equivalences and identities, total and firmly seated in the equality principle, and this way any "union" or "separation" completely stops being pertinent, its pure opportunity is lost. Very surely the matter of this Solar System, an aggregate in partial balance, *is* separating at this same moment of the matter of other places of the galaxy in which there govern different conditions; we could think about conditions of polarization, phenomenon only partially explained since the quantum mechanics ignores questions as the form of the phase or the reason of the definition of the cycle, that only can have relation with a recurrence. Also very surely, the absorption of the light from the most distant corners of the space also has selective criteria, then of separation also, probably related to the previous thing. But all this is already lost conjectures by the same fact to assign them to a frame, the one of physics, modelled entirely in the equality idea; so that it only can offer deformed hypothesis to us. Often it has been believed to eliminate the question of the "internal variables" -in which we do not believe-in the quantum mechanics adducing that such variables, whereas internal, cannot be dependent of the variation of conditions in the exterior. But if we considered to what we have ourselves been referring in the phenomenon of the form in the motion like interface or limit of the interior and the exterior, and whereas defined, eliminating both by unnecessary, we see that these objections are opportune for the quantum mechanics but coarse for the case of the form of the motion in general. The quantum mechanics is therefore consistent with itself but necessarily incomplete with respect to the reality.

Thus, we see that terms such as "to unite and to separate" only have pertinence with respect to the inequality idea: with respect to the equality it is not possible or it is indifferent to separate or to unite anything. And just like we have said of the physics, it can be said of the evolutionary theory, that well would like to define itself —even when it is incapable- like an explanation of the separation of the species or chladogenesis, being able to unite its tree backwards in time, which relegates it to the anecdotal space of "thus was or thus it could be". Because, following with our general presumption, we would finish seeing that in the always virtual separation of the evolutionary branches already are producing unions and contractions between previous spaces of the tree, so that a drag in parallel of the species exists, of the very same form that are taking place in a real tree: from the trunk to each one of the branches we can insert a spiral whose ring is contracted with the force that gives a real module to us, the one of the Golden Section, that appears as well in the spirals of nuclei acids as supra-code -although it is necessary to make notice that there are other planes for the life that the one of the genetics. Without a doubt there are immense spaces of probability to study that would throw numerous surprises, but already would be enough to understand what here implies the simplest and general case.

Let us repeat again that only from the inequality it has some sense to unite and to separate, and therefore, the perpetual activity of the nature. But there is more: only from the point of view of the inequality our own identity, or any other has some sense. How it could be otherwise? It operates already in our thought as form of the motion that it is, and in all its sections. In this respect it is necessary to backslide on the subject that only this inequality equips with content the recurrence. The phenomenon of the frequency expresses a truly circular and trivial fact, that is to say, only that what can disappear finds in conditions for appearing again. But in fact it is far from easy to know if this, to which we called recurrence, is something trivial, because can deceive permanently our expectations of which we considered appearances. The inequality smooth the same sequence of the appearances and disappearances, the same time like principle of succession.

Indeed, the exactly equal waves that fall and elevate in the mind during the concentration, and that we had taken in the beginning like counterpart of mechanical inertia, are referred to the same fact of the recurrence, and not to "the precise" location of the concentration of the attention at a moment without duration of the time, which could not be more unreal. To focus attention on a point means the appearance-and-disappearance of a notion here throughout that interval, appearance-and-disappearance of which it is not possible to say if it is sequential or simultaneous since it is the attention the one that maintains and makes the recurrence possible. Most of us not even we got to realize this, but it is sufficient to show to what extent any problem of continuity or recurrence -not to say all in general- are already present of supreme form in the attention, before in any conceivable content. We cannot know then to what number of levels can exist the recurrence, being decisive that the conscience fills up of the most immediate form the presence or the absence of the object, and revealing itself this way as a different thing from both.

If somebody wanted to respond to that question from Leibniz about why exists in general something rather than nothing, he could see, in terms of the author of that question, that this one is equivalent to ask for the why of the inequality, that is its answer, and thus we can penetrate by not necessarily ontological courses, unless it is had by that the own Leibniz philosophy of or the Indian concept of the being. Why there is something to unite and to separate in the nature? Because there is inequality, and inequalities, and we do not know if both are not the same. Neither the Consciousness have necessarily why to know it, because the consciousness is already the answer.

§ 112 §

It could happen the same with the denominated fundamental forces of the physics. There is no a direct form to know it, since they are modelled on the exclusion of a mean or medium between the action and reaction.

The balance is the sensitivity that exists between the action and reaction; we will never find one more simpler and economic definition. Or vice versa, sensitivity is the tendency to the balance between action and reaction that already as motion is by definition unbalanced.

The constants of coupling or intensity of the so called fundamental forces would be equivalent to that thick signature or form in which the means of balance or sensitivity between opposed actions appear; but as its definition comes already given like force, without specific dependency of the time, does not exist an explicit way of gauge, safe by the mere proportions and their enigmatic reference to the fundamental level, that it does not have differential character unless is introduced as an opportune supplement. Time itself in its synchronous version is only another aspect of this supplement. But thus it is as more veiled is left its nature.

[132]

The degradation of a system always is originated by a loss of its optimal sensitivity, that implies readjustments in the inertial and active components. And the refinement and evolution, that does not demand necessarily the increase of complexity, always go towards a recovery of that optimal of sensitivity that, naturally, also will be varying with time. But the adjustment of

In many biological and complex systems it is noticed how the maximum of stability agrees with the maximum of sensitivity to the perturbations. this optimal is not possible without a consideration of the balance like which we are exposing. Sensitivity is the point to begin with; if we avoided sensitivity, variable by nature, already the reference is lost.

Let us think for example about the phenomenon of the ageing, so immediately associated to losses of energy and corporal mass. However, it is the loss of sensitivity what makes the process irreversible in diverse degrees: we age because we lose sensitivity, and the rest are chain reactions. The action already is also reaction with respect to sensitivity. Clear that this loss is referred to a variable optimal, since in fact with the deterioration and the imbalance a greater sensitivity or hypersensitivity to multiple stimuli is made present. In this game to outline the essence of the not-linearity, of that only apparent absence of proportionality, is synthesized.

§ 113 §

Probably everything would be mechanic if a univocally mechanical definition for a single and simple process existed; but such a thing does not exist. Apart from count on two completely different mechanics —classic and the quantum one—, it does more than one hundred years that Poincaré demonstrated that even considering the classic systems, whenever the principle of least action is satisfied, not many, but infinite possible mechanical explanations exist. This is normal if we considered the exclusion of the medium or mean by the third principle of the mechanics. And in

[133]

spite of everything, it is continued imposing the persistent illusion, even for the more experimented physicist. The problem is always led back towards the last horizon of the fundamental physics, when also it can be seen in the first plane of the landscape.

That landscape of the pictures of prediction —not only in physics, but in economy, ecology, and any discipline that aspires to have mathematical models— is an amalgam of differential equations and statistic, of absolute determinism without place at least for the causality and profiles for immense clouds of ignorance. Of a very comedian way, is to this statistical part, the chance, to which the causality is attributed quite often, in a double exercise of darkening, since the probability states have been selected to a great extent by differential criteria. .We found here again another superposition and another mirage; another impossibility.

With so much emptiness there is space enough for methods that are neither statistical nor differential: for that which allow one more realistic description of the imbalances. And since neither the differential analysis nor the probability allow a causal explanation of the phenomena, although they easily generate that illusion, fits the supposition which any causality or generativity that could emerge from the analysis of the balance only with miss-understanding could seem "mechanical", at least in the sense that now is granted to this word. Therefore, any cause that is worth the trouble of being looked for will be outside mechanics, which by force it has to reveal itself in the mathematical solutions of these systems, which they do not respond to momentary situations, but produced sequentially by successive adjustments. What it is generated in these sequences is the density of the real time; not the synchronous or the ideal time. Or at least, it runs so in parallel that is confused at first sight with it. And we have to arrive at that point in where we have to conclude that, although the variations are infinite, there are always the same principles. .

Even though the tri-modal approach of the equilibrium can not aspire to the deterministic solutions of the differential analysis, what is lost in this aspect is compensated enough with what is won in natural generativity, in the sequence, and therefore, in consequence. Now we are not able to value what this means.

§ 114 §

One could think that the scheme of the *gunas* of the Samkhya is similar to the one of dialectics, to the scheme thesis-antithesis-synthesis; but the dialectic is idealistic, even in its popular and naturalistic versions very previous to the idealism, indeed by its appearance of production of the reality. Also the modern analysis, even being applied faithfully to experimental data, is of idealistic cut from the moment that believes to produce the motion from closed functions with changes in the values or coefficients. Nothing of this has to do with the Samkhya. Although we even found characteristic mathematical structures for the fluctuations with respect to the balance, we would only have a selector of readings, a tuner that allows us to listen better what there is present. A complete and closed description as the one of the analytical functions it would be beforehand irrelevant, would make that listening impossible.

In fact, if there is something primitive that corresponds with the nature of the *gunas*, of sensitivity, the action and reaction, is the same articulation of the language, with his three grammatical persons and their equivalent subject- verb-predicate flow. Not in vain it is adjudge to the name of Patanjali a treatise of grammar, in addition to another one of medicine. The pulse of the cat truly would say "I-eat-sardines" if it did not have much more varied and subtle things to tell us. But it continues being a genuine language because it is articulated, and has to have by force a discreet element to detect, reason for which we have been alluding very insistently to the mathematics of the Golden Mean or Continuous Proportion. Only in a frame like this the non- decidable questions of the last century on semantics and syntax could have value and specific weight.

[135]

Therefore, to speak of the language and the languages of the nature could not be a metaphor —rather the human language must be a poor metaphor of that other language.

Only the overvaluation of the so called classic mechanics and the differential calculus relegated this so natural possibility to the scope —again, purely apparent- of the nonsense. Disappearing the verb and the time of our perception of the nature, also the entity of the other two instances is diluted. Something more than a dimension of the "problem" vanishes therefore, something more than the "depth". Pope tried that *Nature and Nature laws lay hid in the night/ God said: let Newton be! and all was light.* We don´t know what happened to light; but now we can verify that it was at that time that the West lost any ear for the Nature. And it cannot be strange to us that the efforts that now we make to recover it must break through the most abstract dominions, until there where indeed it was lost.

§ 115 §

It have been said thousand times that Galileo moved away to us of the centre of the universe, that the theory of the evolution cleared to us of the pinnacle of the creation, and that the psychoanalysis denied our dominion on our own mind. But, being already lame the first of these three concentric revolutions, the other two, that tried to model their selves to the image and similarity of the mechanics, have been more events of the public opinion and the imaginary that true advances of the knowledge. Neither the mind, nor the life, nor mechanics have been understand or explained. The mechanics continues closing to us the passage to any superior understanding, and thus it is understood the innumerable amount of nonsense and incredible artifices that are postulated like candidates to explain the consciousness, in which it is tried the fourth and definitive "revolution". Nothing of that has the smaller plausibility, and

[136]

the only good thing of so many desperate attempts is to convince to us that something extremely basic has been avoided from the beginning and the principle itself.

Many are the ones that look for the magical concept today that would give potentiality to this last turn: ideas around the computation, the information, the deterministic chaos, the quantum theory and things of the sort. Ideas of last hour to avoid questions about what is generally considered as consolidated. This is quite normal if one thinks that the consciousness is the last and the most conditional thing. Our perception, on the contrary, is that there is very little or nothing to say on this one, and that are the other layers those that would benefit from a new principle. Since nothing really has been explained by them. Even the predictions of the physics, so successful, on objects that are not understood, are based on last instance in the correspondence of the proportion, and not of the causality. From here the "inexplicable effectiveness of the mathematics". This can happen perfectly without doing nothing more than to cut layers or flat films without any other thickness that the possible and imagined relations with other objects, that are also defined in two-dimensional layers.

Only the three-fold concept of fluctuation with respect to the balance can break through from the most fundamental level of physics to the most immediate subjective experiences. From the measurable movement to the qualities, and from a whole to its details. In the landscape of present knowledge there is not and there will not be another possible bridge, and thus it will be while signs of the so called modern science, that historical contingency. The known attempts not even can scratch the reality —it is like make photographs.

§ 116 §

When the Samkhya affirms that there is not another ultimate cause of the variety of the things that *gunas*, which must be

[137]

understood is that truly we cannot understand and assimilate outside the context of the equilibrium or balance. That same process around the balance acts as much in the cognition as in the objects. Therefore, any other understanding, including the one of the habitual analysis, are not but forms more or less far from the centre of the same. Naturally, to no method in itself could correspond the centre; but the differences of direction with respect to it are decisive. It is possible to be confronted or be from behind.

In fact it is the balance the one that assimilate the imbalances, and the one that also makes possible a route beyond the understanding. We not even can assimilate that this earth is an enormous globe with a certain diameter, mass or impulse; in no way we can incorporate or embody those knowledge in ourselves only from the same knowledge.

Nevertheless let us put a simple and perfectly checkable example of *hatha yoga*, the posture of remaining in balance on the head, with this one putting inside a triangle drawn by the forearms. The novice has therefore the opportunity to retake the hard learning of the balance that so much work gave to him being a child and who has arrived to forget almost completely indeed because it has managed. In the beginning, he will be basically at the mercy of inertia; with some practice, it will learn to make the force necessary to resist the oscillations. This will be excessive almost always and bad applied, until gradually it is developed sufficient sensitivity and the unnecessary efforts are saved to the maximum. After a variable period of practice, a more or less perfect union of inertia, force and sensitivity is reached; then not even a special alert on the part of this last one is precise, because it is completely integrated with the other two tendencies. A spontaneous state of suspension takes place *finally*, that nevertheless is the fruit of all the previous efforts and deliberations. Even if we took the work of measure in detail the oscillations that within a circle make the body of the novice and the one of experimented, and for identical deviations of the centre in any direction, would verify the enormous difference throughout the vertical axis with respect to the rigidity of first one and the perfect and synchronous undulation throughout the body of the second for the most effective and coherent accomplishment of the least action. This is an excellent illustration of that lost dimension of the movement to which we alluded; as well as of which we understand like assimilate or incorporate knowledge.

To this general process of concealment in the invisible of the qualities in its total presence is at which it points the experience of the Being in the India philosophy. Such experience allows the participation in the extra-mental dominion with no need of metaphysics.

§ 117 §

It is to note that in cases like this the equilibrium is not and can not be an ideal –infinitesimal- state, but it will be possible always to find it in the empirical and real world for the relevant level. Of course, the most subtle balance may be find at rest, whether the needle is centred or sloped, in every cases that the perturbations don't surpass the own sensibility threshold of the balance. Therefore, this sensibility gauge give us a possibility of realistic definition of the rest and the intrinsic, proper equilibrium of the system, too. Any perturbation will make pass the needle two times by the same point, giving the primary form of the cycle and the recurrence. Possibly, this can be applied to a tri-modal formulation of the quantum of action.

§ 118 §

I hope that the presumption which I have shown with respect to a model or hypothesis that has not been checked at least shall be pardoned; not to mention the integrating pretensions with respect to fields that one so widely ignores. All this is very certain, but it is not but fairly legitimate way to call the attention on a phenomenon, the one of the form in the motion, so absolutely real and fundamental

[139]

that we cannot ignore it without loses the sense of all the others; and if those additional fields did not exist at all, the subject would not lose nor in minimum its own substance and its autonomy, that now has emerged circumstantially by its contrast with the analysis.

§ 119 §

For the Samkhya, as well as for the India philosophy in general, as much the actual infinite as the truly defined and finite escape to the scope of the manifestation. Thus, of the ephemeral world as in motion not even it is possible to be postulated its finitude, nor therefore its complete definition: to realize it would be the only privilege that in this respect we have left. We have tried to speak almost always of indefinite series and indefinite amounts, more than infinite ones; the harmony mathematics and their algorithmic measurement theory seems to be agreed with this yet, and avoids therefore a good part of the dilemmas of the mathematical world.

How it could be perfectly defined the motion? The trimodal or threefold analysis that we have indicated is a way to evade the external references to the own motion, but of this form also tends irretrievably to vanish the external metrics of the space, all the imaginary framework of the representation. Here one is to take care of the sequence of a process forgetting every other thing, perhaps the only legitimate form of abstraction and the most difficult. Sinning the representation always by excess more than by defect, this would not have to be lamented, and until it can be considered like the only real gain. A completely different space for the convergence is generated. And nevertheless, it does not exist nor it can exist the complete mutual incompatibility, since from our point of view we even see how the modes cannot stop to operate in the most net of the mechanics, even leaving apart the inevitable contact with the reality.

[140]

§ 120 §

The logic of the Samkhya leads to us with an irresistible force in the same proportion that we know to resist to the application of the force. So it seems to be the eternal criterion, imposed and to our disposition.

§ 121 §

The search and appeal to the unconditioned exist in all the spheres, not only for the religion. We have all the right and a part of the power to appeal to the unconditioned in the deepest of us; we do not have any right and a part of the power to impose something to others unconditionally. Both plates are always balanced.

§ 122 §

The subject of the Samkhya or the Yoga is to extend the inner space trying not to establish the least differential with the outer space, that is to be respected necessarily. Thus, the difference between the interior and the outside, and the field of reference for the motion stops by the motion itself. Yoga is to penetrate in the limitless using the limits that are given to us, without trying to transgress them or annulling them. The Samkhya is the contemplation of the balance and the Yoga its practice, not existing true difference between both, and being the contemplation the gradual decantation of the purity in the participation. In all the theoretical contemplation that we have made we have tried to guide us by this same practice.

§ 123 §

The subject of the form in the motion, its adjustment, is simply the subject of our insertion in the reality.

§ 124 §

The same modalities, or *gunas*, also are only objects of knowledge in a purely conditional and impermanent way: that is already its form of evolution from the beginning and even without beginnings. Therefore, one can gives the back to them completely without leaving undertaking in any moment . So that, when we said that Patanjali had written its *Yoga-sutras* with the intention of making *gunas* directly contemplable, this only could occur by the way including the salt in the assertion. Certainly, no sort of knowledge forces to contemplate them to us, far from it the one that Samkhya proposes as its crown. This would have to make think about the indescribable state of freedom in which the pure awareness dwells, being the nature of *gunas* simply the nature of the existence of the individual, and being the consciousness the pure universal existence.

It is not necessary to say this doesn't need any attendance from metaphysics.

§ 125 §

The force notion refers to the one of acceleration, that is the change of speed or change within the change; the speed is applied to bodies with mass, being this one an effective quantification of the inertia, that also can be equivalent to the rest. So that all the dynamics or science of the forces is refer to a scalar magnitude *for been able to be applied*; or otherwise the forces would exist immediately in the vacuum. However, as this scalar "component" can not be well modelled by the exigencies of the differential calculus, yes, it results that these forces act in the emptiness of a reality which they do not draw. This is, not being explained the phenomenon of the mass, inertia or the rest, its density with respect to the reality is null. Or said of another form, the thickness of his section or it cuts in the reality is null, unless the imprecision rank is considered of a positive form. That it is, perhaps, which would have to become. So that the only reality of the physics would consist of which it cannot define, not in which it can. This does not have anything of impossible or stranger , but simply, nobody seems to think that it is of some utility to have it in mind.

The same scientific knowledge is of essentially mutative or *rajasic* modality and condition, and it is therefore natural that their support and reference is inertia, the modality that at least partially remains subordinated to it. There is in all this no other mystery nor other evidence. That the inertiality can become equivalent of sensitivity, like we have proposed, is something that from its own nature cannot not even be contemplated; essentially it is forbidden to it, in addition of which it would seem to put in danger its own conception. But it would have to be clear that supporting in inertia the forces they are not less in the air than supporting to us in a self-recurring notion of the impulse, that the only thing that does is to define the density and thickness in the section of chosen reality. So that physics cannot avoid to be as much in the air or as conditional as our balance, and the only alarming would seem to be the absence of conscience of it. The remissions of the acceleration to the speed and this one to the rest are independent of the time; here it is all the fault with respect to the reality, and from here all the vain efforts to fill something that cannot be heaped.

It does not seem very consequent then to assimilate inertia with nullity, the one of the rest, for example, since if all the physics is derived from this, we do not know why at some moment would have to stop being nothing; to assimilate it with the principle of minimum action, being quantified it in reference to the value of *Phi* like Grejzdelsky does, seems to be justified and to suppose something more than a semantic question. Being so far from being a simple nothing, inertia only can be conceived like least action, also in harmony with the notion of modification or impulse like change of the moment. The not-nullity of inertia is the revocation or ousting of the reversible time of mechanics.

What confers stability then to things is not inertia, but the least action, independently of which we consider it like quantum, law, or principle, since it is itself the one that makes the translations between possible levels of the reality, like before made inertia with its own incapacity. That the least action principle is the only guarantee of the theoretical stability of the things do not speaks us as much of the fragility of the reality like of the fragility of the theory itself: therefore, it is for our conscience a magnificent index.

This would suppose a definitive step to superpose us to the ideality of our definitions, perhaps so that someday we could pose legitimately what has to do inertia with the imitation, the habit, the perception and the variation of a stimulus; and which is the sort of possible continuity between physical, biological, and psychological notions —although the true question is that other criteria of separation that the imaginary ones never existed. We now have a suitable translator principle. This principle seems to trascend the notion of territory in anyone of the specialities, being this perhaps its happier utility.

However, in all this we follow without realize that the application of the asymmetric theory of the measurement to the motion subtlety changes but radically the whole definition of the reality. **Any order of precision that is not self-refer to its own terms already is imaginary,** because as for the rest neither its imprecision, **for want of a proper form**, it does not talk about anything but a mere deficiency. Will be finally this one the principle of adjustment or truth of all the theories at the moment handled? It is necessary to consider all this very seriously, since it affects something more than to the criterion of measurement or the metric. Any more selective form of space or representation will have to emerge from which is raised here. The more perceptive aspect of the reality is also the most constructive, and therefore, this fundamentally affects to the harmony and coherence between the different specialities and disciplines, final destiny of all the diseconomies. Let us repeat it: the precision criteria that we usually handle are fundamentally imaginary, because they lack explicit degrees to define its inclusion in the reality. These explicit degrees are not necessary, since they can be contemplated of inherent form; but for the present state of things, in which this tends to be made less and less, they become a pure function of adjustment.

The self-reference is the reality criterion, the translation principle, the only truth that lies in the idea of self-organization. This is something natural and inexcusable, not a vitiated application of an abstract logic. If it has seemed a vitiated resource speech more than nothing of how vitiated are resources incapable to make a exact use of this fact. The test of this fact is the degree of independence or economy with respect to the formalisms, and we are those that supports the test.

The logic of the self-reference or inequality favours the thickening of things; the one of equivalence, favours the dissolution. The contact or confrontation of both is inevitable.

§ 126 §

Consciousness does not have memory.

§ 127 §

It is to sorry that the deepest theoreticians of the physics and other disciplines that try to seize in the reality often say that perhaps we will never understand the world because we are not the intelligent enough. First of all, by the absurd arrogance that such affirmations imply, assuming that the world has to be comprehensible, and in addition by intelligence, and a very concrete and formal intelligence in particular. By these words it rather speaks the disorientation and the ignorance, in individual and general, in addition to those pretensions so little promising for the knowledge; and also speak the modes by the people. It would be to wish that intelligence served to illuminate our ignorance more than to illuminate our fragmentary knowledge; in this respect our

[145]

hypothesis or symbol does not have any integrating pretension, although they only seem to draw it the possible effects.

And what would happen if we did not understand the world simply because we are not worthy of it?

To appeal to intelligence already is a form to cry.

§ 128 §

The symbolic model of the balance or the Samkhya already incorporates the external means in the processes, liberating the problem of the reference. To define from the outside the questions of evolution and balance, or the relevant ranks of precision, are the improper thing. Now it is to see until where it takes to us to try a proper definition of the motion and the modifications adhering to the proper form, locating itself in the middle of the conditions. In any case, the distinctions between the mechanic or non-mechanic, the determinism and the non-determinism, become arbitrary and irrelevant, because they admit indefinite degrees that never are incumbent on to that question, that already is raised from outside. The intellect is one more of those degrees, simultaneously that its refinement, which indeed leaves back the complexity of the states, if it is certain that the essence of the distillation is the essence.

As far as the consciousness, it is still more certain that it is not the object of any discipline. If some grant possibility to that delirium, is by supposing it like the most highly conditional, while the un-conditionality of the physical laws is assumed. But the situation is exactly the opposite: any physical data, including the measurement of the rest, already involves a modification, an asymmetry *of* the space and the time.

The Vedanta could not express it better: If the consciousness can not explain itself, what thing could explain it?

[146]

The real is the existence. The existence is the consciousness. The consciousness is the real thing. That is the triple affirmation in which it is summarized the Vedanta and the Samkhya, a triple identity as existential as absolute. Empty? May be: consciousness is completely indifferent to the fullness or the vacuity. Consciousness, already we said it, does not have memory, not at all paradoxical affirmation that anyone can verify by means of the portion that corresponds to him. An affirmation in which lie very considerable possibilities.

If the consciousness does not have memory, in that exact measure the consciousness is will; if the consciousness is will, in that exact measure the consciousness does not need to know. That exact measurement that we are speaking about is the conation, that it does not have to be confused necessarily with the will; then if there is conation, the consciousness is only intelection, and if there is none, the consciousness remains undivided in these terms and indifferent to them. This is an example of something which not even needs to be thought; then the terms fall here by themselves, without thinking about how we could take part in them. And exactly in the same way but in very different measure it happens to us with the equations. We are not invited to think about it, but to verify it. The consciousness does not have memory. With as much disorientation, we can not think in a better indicator of the "location" of the consciousness, for those who want to look for it.

For those who please to quantify, an unobjectionable definition of the consciousness is that it folds the three modalities in anything, corresponding this way to the triple previous affirmation. This triple identity does not have sequence, and therefore it is unattainable for the logic or the mathematics, that sometimes believe to be in the ultimate degree of the simplicity, the un- conditionality or even the elegance. In fact, the mathematical forms are only appeal to other forms, and would be enough to have the sufficient attention, with no need of a mathematical intellect, to realize that they are not more near from the eternity than the first or the last of the words pronounced by the man. The opposite is a presumption, motivated nevertheless by the implicit movement in the aspiration, more than by the execution or the assumption of conscience; therefore, and like all movement of the language, it has a excusable necessity.

So that the triple identity of the Vedanta offers us like a space for the contemplation to our whole disposition, since in no case it imposes nothing to us. It is the maximum and the minimum that can be said. But it is also a proclamation and the testimony of most legitimate of the conquests, because it have been made in the pure conditionality, of which all the forms depend.

In any case, to mention the consciousness is not absolutely inopportune indeed because of how acute begins to be our conscience of the insufficiency of all the formal systems, and by ours very justified distrust on the fascination of all the theoretical abysses. We can assume this in opposite direction of the rhetoric and the brutality, who already are made present in the same intellect.

Being the intellect adhesion before any other thing, if it does not realize that only lets take, he is already lost, and only through the experience it will be able to recover of that loss, whenever it is made, and non only with the intellect, the sufficient effort. This is fundamental subject for the Samkhya, because the modalities exist indifferently like liberation and experience source, without excluding both terms safe by the own modes. The Samkhya affirms that the liberation is the identity of the intellect and the consciousness: but this identity does not belong to the intellect, because all this, at least for it, is conditioned by defined degrees or modes.

Properly speaking, the consciousness does not belong to us, we only can hope to correspond to us with it. And here takes root any possible freedom far from all rhetoric. That is to say, there is no another one. The rest is only compulsion, and the lucidity of the intellect, always lent, out of the consciousness already is superimposition and blindness whatever will be the level in which it appears. Therefore the consciousness is neither a rhetorical subject nor a problem of location, but the only reference and the only means of evolution in the real time. Real time is consciousness without memory.

APPENDIX-A PROBLEM

We would like to shortly expose the problem again, in a non technical form, in the way to a better future approach:

The wave of the physiological pulse has a cushioned profile that is essential for its study and characterization.

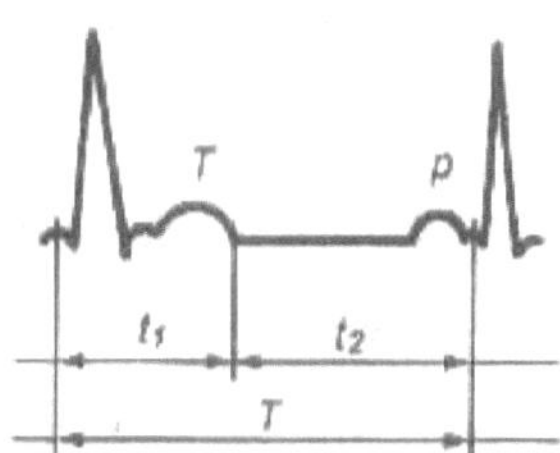
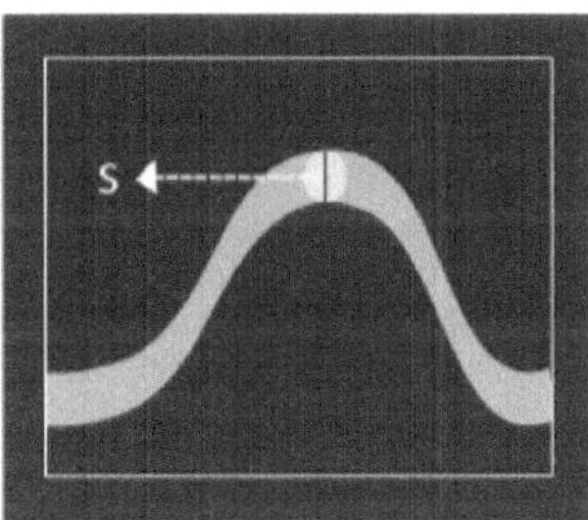

Now let us consider that damping or amplitude of the signal like a natural index of a hypothetical inequality or mean between the action and reaction, or the kinetic and the potential energy of the system. **The time** between the action and the reaction must be different from zero. This hypothesis is specially permissible for a complex system of biological type, in which the reaction to the stimuli hardly can be considered immediate. We can describe this behaviour in its simpler form by the oscillation of a balance with inertiality or **sensitivity**, that is to say, with a time of reaction for the operations of adding or removing weights.

Let us suppose that the amplitude of the signal is an indicator of that time of reaction or sensitivity (*S*) of the system.

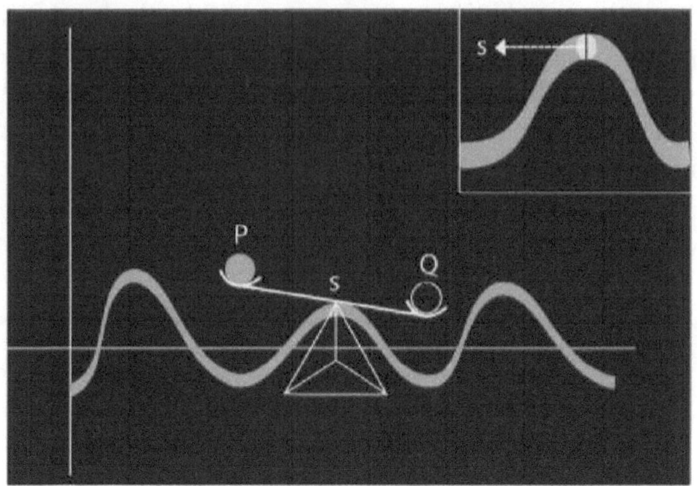

Being the weights Q and P mediated by *S*, the three can be defined as impulses *(F x t)*, where the applied force is dependent of the time — that is to say, do not exist forces that can be applied independently of the time, which also is specially pertinent in a behaviour like the one of the pulse—. Therefore, the values of impulse of Q and P are based on *S*.

The potential sum of kinetic and potential energy (Q + P) can decrease or increase throughout the time, if we suppose a disease or an improvement. We can suppose, nevertheless, that the total sum of (Q+P+ *S*) has to remain equal to the unit (Q+P+S) = 1. In a certain way, the inertiality or sensitivity of the balance is equal to *the internal* energy of the system, so that (Q+P+*S*) = (Q+P+I), although *S*, the sensitivity, also can be an index of the external environment and of how it affects the system. *S* also is a specific indicator of the degradation or disorder of the system; another form for detecting the entropy.

There are pathological increases of sensitivity. On the other hand, in biological systems the "maximum" of sensitivity usually agrees with the maximum of stability. Then we have the problem of how defining here the maximums, minimums, as well as the optimal value of *S*. The same stability in dynamic systems is also referred to this last component.

[150]

- The time interval St > 0 comprehends an asymmetry and a propensity towards Q or P, and possibly also towards the past or the future of the system, that eventually can balance; if there is no asymmetry the average values of the amplitude would tend to a simple line for the curve, instead of a band of irregular width, and there would not be substantial difference with the habitual descriptions.

- Can we cover therefore the complete curve with the wave of the pulse –with its whole form and its thickness- with a group of discreet weights?

- May we give different values and groups of weights for Q and P? Determining S the time of reaction, the proper values of impulse *(F x t)* for Q and P always depend on the first one. It would have to exist therefore a generative or causal order in the changes of Q, P, and S. But it happens that also S is variable. Lack the system all kind of solutions if Q, P and S are variable?

- Although there were no simple solutions, we always can fit the system with the value of S that gives us the measurement. The experimental value is the reference; if this value is momentary, will diverge very quickly in the time, losing the validity in a few moments. It is to be noted nevertheless that the time intervals do not tend to zero, nor the values are purely instantaneous, like in the classic differential systems, and that is the reason for which certain causal or generative nexus between the past and the future is possible, which it is not possible in classic systems. But this causal order only can talk about to the balance and the dynamic adjustments that make it possible.

- The cycle or period with *pi* base (π), each beat, naturally continues being an operator for the rotation of operations allowed by the balance. The differences of profile between a pulsation and another one must respond to the inequality of times and the consequent compensation for the operations.

[151]

- It seems to be that the ternary systems of weighting are often optimal to make a minimum number of operations. It has the *Phi* constant (Φ) = 1,618... and his associate values some specific relation with this class of systems?

- What class of predictions allows this class of description? What elements allow characterize in the temporary evolution?

- A system like this is mechanic in the most general sense, that is to say, in the sense expressed by the principle of least action. This principle, for the classic systems, allows infinity of partial mechanical explanations, i.*e.*, it is not univocal. This is a logical consequence of its formulation: when lacking explicit means, it makes possible all kind of mechanics means like explanation, without affecting the general behaviour of the system. Do allow an additional dimension or variable like the one we consider a more univocal explanation and a greater concretion for the principle of least action? Do allow a wider base for this principle? Can we make specific and deepen the idea of the balance?

- If this description can be applied to the biological pulse, also it can be applied to other periodic biological signals, although initially the signal would not be registered with such elements that in the pulse. Nevertheless, a transformation without the experimental measurement will only have probabilistic character, since S is the reference for the proper values of Q and P.

- In economy, the transactions are asymmetric, as demonstrate the graphics of supply and demand. Nevertheless these not show a specific form in the temporary graphs. We can take like example the stock-market operations, which involve a time of transaction very related to the momentary slope of the curve of quotations. This it is a typical example of time of reaction for complex systems. Nevertheless, it can be that this time of reaction is not directly dependent of the slope of the curve, but on the contrary is the initial factor of reference in the determination of the values and the operations. It is possible to say the same for other many curves of temporary evolution, like for example the climatic curves, in spite of the well-known differences between the systems. Anyway, we don't know yet if this description affects more significantly to the prediction or the understanding of these systems, or both.

- To what extent this model can become general for complex systems? The concept of balance is absolutely fundamental, weather in economy, ecology, biology, psychology or physics. Is S a true synthesis of the non-linearity of the system, that only allows to be kept awake by successive degrees? These degrees can not be merely methodical steps of approach, also can be inherent to the nature of the problem. In fact, the degrees and shades seem to be inherent to the nature, but the differential description does not allow an appropriate place to them.

- In physics, for the classic systems, we have a time of reaction equal to zero ($St= 0$).It would rather mean this that its sensitivity is the maximum, or that is null?

- However, this is clearly an idealization. For quantum objects a minimum time of action or reaction is necessary. Nevertheless, the quantum of action, defined as energy x cycle x second, does not give us any possible content of operations for the unit of a cycle. Can be the quantum of action redefined according to our three components?

BIBLIOGRAPHY — REFERENCES

Swami Hariharananda Aranya, 2000. *Yoga philosophy of Patanjali with bhasvati*. University of Calcutta.

Simon Weil, 2001. *Cuadernos*. Editorial Trotta.

Alexis Jardines Chacón, 2000. *El enigma del movimiento*. Biblioteca Nueva, Madrid.

Miguel Iradier, 2001. *La hija del capitán Starbuck (Hurqualya)*.

Biblioteca Nueva, Madrid.

Alexey Stakhov. *Museum of Harmony and Golden Section (Alexey Stakhov web site)* www.goldenmuseum.com

Koichiro Matsuno. *Resurrection of Cartesian Physics*

Domingo S. Acosta. *The inertial mass*

Paul Marmet. List of Papers and Web Sites www.newtonphysics.on.ca